Penguin Critical Studies

Much Ado About Nothing

Dr Roger Sales is a lecturer in English Studies at the University of East Anglia. He was formerly a research assistant with BBC TV and has edited two volumes of *Shakespeare in Perspective* (1982 and 1985), which contain television and radio talks on all of Shakespeare's plays. His other main publications include *English Literature in History 1780–1830: Pastoral and Politics* and, in the Penguin Critical Studies series, *Tom Stoppard: Rosencrantz and Guildenstern are Dead* (1988).

Penguin Critical Studies
Advisory Editor:
Bryan Loughrey

William Shakespeare

Much Ado About Nothing

Roger Sales

Penguin Books

PENGUIN BOOKS

Published by the Penguin Group
27 Wrights Lane, London W8 5TZ, England
Viking Penguin Inc., 40 West 23rd Street, New York, New York 10010, USA
Penguin Books Australia Ltd, Ringwood, Victoria, Australia
Penguin Books Canada Ltd, 2801 John Street, Markham, Ontario, Canada L3R 1B4
Penguin Books (NZ) Ltd, 182–190 Wairau Road, Auckland 10, New Zealand

Penguin Books Ltd, Registered Offices: Harmondsworth, Middlesex, England

First published as a Penguin Masterstudy 1987
Reprinted as a Penguin Critical Study 1989
10 9 8 7 6 5 4 3 2 1

Made and printed in Great Britain by
Richard Clay Ltd, Bungay, Suffolk
Filmset in Monophoto Times

For Victor Poole, with thanks

Contents

Textual Note and Acknowledgements

The quotations from *Much Ado* are taken from the new Penguin Shakespeare edition. I have followed the stage directions in this edition, with the exception of those that refer to the masked ball. Quotations from other plays by Shakespeare are also taken from the New Penguin Shakespeare editions. I found A.R. Humphrey's Arden Shakespeare edition of *Much Ado* particularly helpful when working on complicated passages. I have tried, wherever possible, to use standard modern editions for the quotations from other Renaissance writers. Where these were not available, I have usually modernized the spelling to make the arguments more accessible. The bibliography lists some of the books and articles which have influenced my own reading of the play. I have not, however, included detailed references to them in my argument. I would therefore like to take this opportunity to acknowledge my debt to them. I have also learnt a great deal from discussing *Much Ado* with Victor Poole, with whom I worked for a number of years on the BBC TV *Shakespeare in Perspective* programmes, Tony Gash from the University of East Anglia and my wife Anne. Finally, I am very grateful to the advisory editors of this series, Stephen Coote and Bryan Loughrey, for their perceptive comments on an early draft for this book.

Part One: Introduction

1 Plays Within Plays

Much Ado About Nothing opens on an appropriately mock-heroic note. A languid messenger has just arrived in Messina with news of Don Pedro of Arragon's military victory over his petulant brother, Don John. Leonato, the Governor of Messina, swaps pleasantries with this unpleasant flunkey. His niece, Beatrice, flouts their diplomatic celebration of war by mocking Benedick, one of Don Pedro's gallants. The scene is now set for the triumphant return of the conquering heroes. Leonato welcomes them to his house with extravagant gestures of hospitality. Beatrice and Benedick welcome each other with equally extravagant gestures of hatred. The dashing young soldier, Claudio, eyes up Leonato's daughter, Hero. He confesses his love for her to Benedick, but the response from the older and wiser soldier is a predictably cynical and scornful one. Don Pedro is, however, more sympathetic to his young protégé's plight and agrees to woo Hero for him. The plan is for Don Pedro to impersonate Claudio at the masked ball and declare his love for Hero. He is then, playing himself, to approach Leonato for permission for the young couple to marry. A garbled version of this plan is brought to Leonato by his aged brother, Antonio. They are under the false impression that Don Pedro, far from playing the part of go-between, wants Hero for himself. A truer version reaches the ears of the defeated and disgruntled Don John, who had been brought back to Messina in the shadow of his victorious brother. He and his accomplices snap up the overheard conversational trifle and fashion it into a scheme to get their own back on Don Pedro and Claudio.

Leonato, revelling in his role as host, throws a banquet and lays on a masked ball. Antonio has already warned Hero that Prince Don Pedro may approach her during this ball. Leonato tries to make sure that Hero knows the lines appropriate for her part as aspiring princess, but everybody finds it difficult to get a word in edgeways as Beatrice is playing the part of disdainful lady with no interest in any marriage. The ball commences with the gentlemen masked and the ladies unmasked. Hero takes a turn with Don Pedro, still under the misapprehension that he woos for himself. Beatrice and Benedick are amongst the couples who tread a measure together. Beatrice, pretending not to recognize her old adversary, abuses him to his mask. Don John has distinctly unfestive reasons for becoming a late arrival at this ball. He plays his own variation on the theme of masks and deceptions by pretending to mistake Claudio for

Benedick. He then starts the rumour that brother Don Pedro is really looking after himself. The masked ball has not produced harmony. Benedick is determined to get even with Beatrice and Claudio is thrown into dejection and self-doubt by the news of his patron's low cunning. Don Pedro eventually puts him out of his misery by triumphantly declaring that everything has gone according to the original plan. Arrangements are made for the marriage of the gauche Claudio and the silent Hero. The only problem now appears to be how to pass the time before the wedding. Contrary to popular mythology, the rich are seldom idle. Don Pedro fancies staging another performance in the part of go-between and decides that it would be a spiffing wheeze to have Beatrice and Benedick fall in love with each other. He has no difficulty in casting Leonato, Claudio and Hero in supporting roles. Meanwhile, as they say, Don John is planning a comeback performance. His oily sidekick, Borachio, tells him that Claudio's marriage can be prevented if Hero is dishonoured. The plot here is for Borachio himself and Hero's maid, Margaret, to play the parts of Hero and a lover, with Claudio strategically placed as the audience. Borachio is more than a good friend of Margaret's and so anticipates no problems in casting her for the part. Don John, in his role as theatrical impresario, thinks that the price is right at a thousand ducats for such a play. The sportive Don Pedro and his troupe of unpaid actors are now ready to stage their performance for Benedick. Everybody in Messina is suspicious of what is being said behind their backs, so it is quite natural for Benedick to whip behind a tree when he hears Don Pedro, Leonato and Claudio talking about him. At first he thinks he might be being played for a sucker when the talk is all about Beatrice's undisclosed passion for him. The presence of the respectable, elderly Leonato persuades him that he is not being led up the garden path. The actors conclude their improvised play and leave Benedick to respond to it. He decides, remarkably quickly, that he must do the decent thing and return Beatrice's love. He is unable, after all, to be the founding father of a long line of bachelors. Their new relationship gets off to a bad start. Beatrice enters, cued by Don Pedro, with the prosaic news that dinner is served. Benedick tries to pluck significant hints from her offhand commands.

Hero, also being stage-managed by Don Pedro, plans the sequel to this play with her two maids, Margaret and Ursula. Parts are quickly rehearsed before Beatrice furtively takes up her position as the audience. Hero and Ursula then go dangerously close to the top in performances designed to convince Beatrice that Benedick is eating his heart out for her. The actresses exit and Beatrice quickly accepts their illusion as reality. Speaking in very laboured verse, she declares that Benedick's love must be returned.

If love transforms her from a sharp talker into a halting versifier, the change in Benedick is just as dramatic. The poor gallant is not as he has been. He dresses more flamboyantly than usual and has had his beard shaved off in deference to Beatrice's professed dislike of such coarseness. He is now equipped to play the Latin lover, although an attack of toothache hinders his performance. Don John plays the part of the honest, plain-speaking soldier when he tells Don Pedro and Claudio that Hero is not as she seems. Despite his bad track record and the fact that Claudio now knows that he told a lie at the masked ball, he has very little difficulty in persuading his audience to take up their positions in the orchard outside Hero's window at midnight. Dogberry, Verges and the members of the Watch appear for the first time and prepare themselves for a hard night's inactivity. As the Watch bed themselves down for a couple of hours of unearned rest, Borachio begins his rambling confession to Conrade, another of Don John's henchmen, about the part he has just played in dishonouring Hero. Once again, a concealed audience on stage, the Watch, listen to somebody else's conversation. The Watch eventually decide to get in on the act and, astonishing even themselves, surprise these two villains. Hero is blissfully unaware of the nocturnal activities and inactivities. She prepares for her wedding as if nothing is wrong. As so often in the play, fashion is the fashionable talk. She is helped to dress by the disloyal Margaret, who feels that a strong line in sexual innuendo is also appropriate for the occasion. Beatrice is not much help as her lovesickness has taken the form of a common cold. Dogberry and Verges make a stately entrance at the Governor's residence to explain the details of the arrest. Leonato is far too preoccupied with his daughter's wedding to have the patience to tease out the meaning of the circumlocutory officer. He dashes off, ordering Dogberry to examine the prisoners himself.

Claudio and Don Pedro believe Don John's craftily constructed illusion to be the reality. They go through the motions of fetching Hero to church and letting the marriage service begin, but this is all a mask. They have already decided to shame her in public. Indeed, this was their contingency plan even before they had witnessed Margaret's performance as Hero. Their speeches are thus well rehearsed. Hero faints and is given up for dead when confronted by the polished accusations of this accomplished double act. Nobody is willing to defend her honour and Margaret, who might have put the record straight, is not present. Don Pedro and Claudio, cued by Don John, sweep out of the church leaving confusion in their wake. Leonato, in a histrionic performance which nearly equals that of Claudio, is relieved that his daughter is no longer alive to bring shame and dishonour to his name. The Friar nevertheless proclaims her innocence, more on the basis of clerical intuition than hard evidence. Hero recovers from her death-like trance and is put through a gentle cross-examination by him. Benedick, who did not join his old friends in their dramatic exit, also attempts to clear her name. The Friar suggests that one way to proclaim her innocence would be to continue to proclaim her death. This would have the added benefit of making Claudio repent his actions. At the very least, the Friar argues, a 'dead' Hero could begin a new life somewhere else without too much difficulty. Benedick urges Leonato to accept this scenario. The Friar thus takes over as the author of the plays within the play. Beatrice and Benedick are left alone in the church. It is the first time they have been alone since becoming convinced of each other's love. Benedick's profession of love does not, however, meet with a totally sympathetic response from Beatrice, who has been crying because of the cruel way in which Hero has been treated. If Benedick really loves her and is not just acting a part, she claims, then he ought to kill Claudio. Somewhat reluctantly, he agrees to play the part of the avenger. Hero's examination in the church is now followed by that of Borachio and Conrade in the court of law. Point, counterpoint is very much the point of the play. Dogberry is resplendent in one of his gowns and, with considerable assistance from the Sexton, stumbles across the truth of the matter. He also gets very steamed up at being called an ass by Conrade. Leonato, who has still not heard the results of Dogberry's deliberations, has nevertheless been convinced that Hero is innocent. So when he and Antonio meet a rather waspish Don Pedro and Claudio, harsh words are exchanged. Antonio tries to interest Claudio in a duel. This comedy routine is interrupted by the arrival of a slightly more serious contender for the honour of killing Claudio. Benedick rejects his former friends by refusing to join in their wordplay and issues his challenge. He also tells them in passing that Don John has fled. The game is almost up. Dogberry, with a great deal of help from the penitent Borachio, confirms Don John's guilt to Don Pedro and Claudio and then to Leonato. Benedick, too self-conscious in his new role as duellist and sonneteer, adopts a more realistic approach to Beatrice. Don Pedro and Claudio, now completely convinced of Hero's innocence, engage in an elaborate, nocturnal ritual of repentance at her tomb. This is part of the play authored by the Friar and now stage-managed by Leonato, as is Claudio's promise to marry one of Hero's cousins. Another formal masquerade takes place, although this time it is the ladies who wear the masks. Claudio takes his new bride sight unseen and it is only then that she reveals herself to be Hero. Benedick asks Beatrice to unmask so that he can propose to her. He has already broached the subject with both Leonato and the Friar.

These two lovers approach marriage in their own way through gentle mockery of their previous antagonism and are not thrown off course by revelations about the plays that Don Pedro staged to bring them together. Benedick celebrates by leading the pre-nuptial dance which, unlike the masked ball, establishes harmony. There are some potential discordant notes at the end of these plays: the news of Don John's capture, Don Pedro's exclusion from the wedding festivities and the possibility that Beatrice might have been tamed. They are, nevertheless, drowned by more festive sounds. Dogberry and the Watch are officially excluded from such high-society celebrations but, at the end of Elizabethan and Jacobean productions anyway, would have been waiting in the wings to jig on for their own particular brand of festivity. The theatre audience, which has been eavesdropping on the eavesdroppers throughout, is now left to respond to the plays that have been performed.

Part Two: Contexts

2 The Moment of *Much Ado*

First performances

The first performances of *Much Ado* can be dated quite precisely. The play was not included in a reasonably reliable list of Shakespeare's works which was drawn up in September 1598. Yet it successfully established itself in the repertoire of Shakespeare's company, the Lord Chamberlain's Men, some time within the next six months. The main evidence for such dating is the fact that the part of Dogberry was written for Will Kempe, the leading comic actor of the day, who left the company at the beginning of 1599. The names of Kempe and Dogberry are interchangeable in the quarto, or published version of the play, which appeared in 1600. This edition was based on a relatively 'clean' and trustworthy manuscript, possibly even Shakespeare's own copy. So *Much Ado* almost certainly had its first performance some time between the autumn of 1598 and the spring of 1599. Given the difficulties that surround the dating of some of the other plays, it is quite an achievement to be able to pin one of them down to within six months.

It is a pity, however, that further precision is not possible. A celebrated theatrical event took place during these particular six months, but it is difficult to relate it to the first performances of *Much Ado*. The Theatre, which had been built by James Burbage in 1576, had become the Lord Chamberlain's Men's more or less permanent base. The landlord made difficulties about the renewal of the ground lease, so the company was forced to transfer their productions to The Curtain. The actors returned to The Theatre on the night of 28 December 1598 to dismantle the building itself, which was legally their property, and to ferry it across the river to Bankside. They then built a new theatre, The Globe, with these old materials and the rest is, as they say, history. It would be interesting to know whether *Much Ado* was written specifically for The Globe, perhaps even for the opening performances there. Speculation is not required, however, to establish the more general points that it was written for public, as opposed to coterie or private, performance and that at some time it became part of the Lord Chamberlain's Men's successful repertoire at The Globe.

Other new plays by Shakespeare which helped to establish The Globe's reputation round about the same time include *Henry V*, *Julius Caesar*, *As*

You Like It, Twelfth Night and *Hamlet*. Although *Much Ado* comes out of the same period of Shakespeare's career as two of the 'festive comedies' (*As You Like It* and *Twelfth Night*), many critics see it as a one-off comedy rather than belonging to an easily identifiable group. Indeed, the suggestion is quite often made that, if *Much Ado* has to be grouped with other plays, then it is more at home with later 'problem' comedies such as *All's Well That Ends Well* than it is with the 'festive' comedies. This account of the play will challenge such suggestions on two counts. First of all, it will establish that the 'comic climate' of the play is festive rather than problematic, light rather than dark. Secondly, it will show that in trying to locate *Much Ado* it makes more sense to go back into the 1590s rather than forward into the 1600s. The play has a number of interesting similarities with the broad, almost farcical, comedy in *The Taming of the Shrew* or *The Merry Wives of Windsor*. It also needs to be related to the 'festive' comedies of the 1590s. The suggestion that it belongs to a group of 'love-comedy game' plays, which also includes *Love's Labour's Lost* and *As You Like It*, is much more helpful than attempts to classify it as a 'dark' comedy.

Much Ado has always been a favourite with theatre audiences. Elizabethan theatre companies only published a play to register and protect their copyright. Once this had been done, it became harder for rival companies to get away with performances based on pirated texts. Publication therefore provides an indication of a play's popularity. A play was not published or 'stayed' so that it could be read or studied as well as performed, as might be the case today, but mainly to prevent slick operators from cashing in on its success. Elizabethan theatrical waters, like those of today's video industry, were infested with sharks and pirates. The title page of the 1600 quarto of *Much Ado* describes it as having been 'sundrie times publickly acted by the right honourable the Lord Chamberlaine his servants'. This was a truly remarkable achievement in such a relatively short space of time, as Elizabethan theatres did not offer continuous runs or even limited seasons. If a play were to establish itself, it had to do so through a much more occasional mode of theatrical production. Elizabethan companies, which during their peak season offered a play six afternoons in the week, might well choose to do a different play each afternoon. Their repertory system was more extensive than is common today. *Much Ado*'s popularity was not short-lived. The admittedly sketchy evidence suggests that it remained a favourite with audiences right up to the closing of the theatres by the Puritans in 1642. Although Shakespeare's plays in their original form were not popular during the Restoration, *Much Ado* had re-established its popularity, with both actors and audiences, by the mid eighteenth century. Despite its critical neglect, it has never lost its theatrical appeal. Too much should not be read into the fact that it was one of the many plays performed at King James's Court in 1613 during the festivities that accompanied the marriage of Princess Elizabeth and the Elector Palatine. Its choice confirms its popularity, but should not be taken to imply that it is necessarily a sophisticated comedy of manners, which celebrates courtly attitudes and aspirations. Its 'comic climate' probably needs to be established in relation to its almost continuous popularity on the public stage. This at least allows for the possibility that, far from being celebratory, it derives its theatrical strength from a parody or even burlesque of courtly behaviour. Critics have not paid sufficient attention to the ways in which *Much Ado* pokes fun at the art of coarse courtiership.

Significance of title

Shakespeare's comedies almost define themselves as such by their catchy, throwaway titles: *Much Ado About Nothing, As You Like It* and *Twelfth Night, or what you will* being obvious examples. At their simplest level, these titles merely offer an audience a general forecast of 'comic climate'. A few critics, following the lead of one of the Victorian editors of *Much Ado*, suggest that, given Elizabethan pronunciation, it ought to be known as *Much Ado About Noting*. As will be apparent, the action of the play certainly revolves around a series of failures at noting, or judging, correctly. An alternative Elizabethan meaning of noting, to call into question or disgrace, also fits quite comfortably. Yet to base such readings too closely around the title itself seems a classic case of interpretation in search of justification. It is better to stick with a consideration of what nothing might have meant to the Elizabethans. The most obvious associations were sexual ones: a 'thing' was familiar slanguage for male genitalia so nothing, or 'no thing', carried pejorative references to female genitalia. Hamlet uses the word in this sense to Ophelia immediately before the Mousetrap, or play within the play:

HAMLET   *Do you think I meant country matters?*
OPHELIA   *I think nothing, my lord.*
HAMLET   *That's a fair thought – to lie between maids' legs.*
OPHELIA   *What is, my lord?*
HAMLET   *Nothing.*

(III. ii. 125–30)

23

The same sexual associations are being played upon when Benedick declares his love for Beatrice after Hero's denunciation:

BENEDICK *I do love nothing in the world so well as you; is not that strange?*
BEATRICE *As strange as the thing I know not.*

(IV. i. 264–6)

For the Elizabethans, if not for Victorian editors, the title probably offered both a sexual statement and, more importantly, the promise of more sexual jokes to come. Benedick and Beatrice fulfil such expectations, even during the play's potentially sombre moments.

This sexual interpretation of 'no thing' quickly shades over into the kind of paradoxes so beloved by Renaissance writers and audiences. If 'nothing' lies 'between maids' legs', how is it possible for 'something' like Hamlet himself to exist? There are further twists in the linguistic maze. 'Nothing' by definition ought to be beyond the world of definition, but the very act of labelling it as 'nothing' automatically transforms it into 'something'. A similar set of problems attach themselves to 'infinity'. Paradoxically, 'infinity' becomes finite by being referred to as 'infinity'. The unknown and unknowable can only become accessible by becoming 'something' it is not. 'Nothing' thus becomes associated with, not total absence, but the active presence of qualities such as chaos and disorder. So it is possible to play a more complicated variation on the sexual theme. Female sexuality, far from being 'nothing', becomes an active and activating chaos, as indeed it is for Hamlet himself, King Lear and Posthumus in *Cymbeline*. According to this hysterical interpretation, 'every thing' might eventually come to 'no thing'.

Shakespeare's Sonnets play with and around these and similar paradoxes. *Much Ado* may, however, also be concerned with yet another meaning of nothing. The question Shakespeare might be playfully posing in the title is whether the theatre, and theatricality, is something or nothing. In other words, whether the playwright is a benign creator on the side of order, or an anarchic destroyer on the side of chaos. This admittedly speculative reading of the title needs to be set in the context of Elizabethan attitudes to the theatre. Some of Shakespeare's contemporaries, particularly Puritan preachers and City worthies, had little doubt that the theatre was a source of anarchy rather than culture. They were afraid of large crowds, amongst whom contagious diseases and ideas might spread unchecked. The London theatres were usually closed at the first whiff of plague and then kept shut for longer than was probably necessary, as they were for instance in 1593. Shakespeare's enemies were also worried by the way in which afternoon performances encouraged idleness, or nothing, rather than industry, or something. It was not just a fear that the shoemakers were taking too many holidays. It was also felt that, by mixing with the 'light and lewd' persons who were supposed to frequent playhouses, they too would be dragged down into the abyss. Matters were not helped by the fact that the playhouses were only a caution's throw away from the brothels. Many of these criticisms of the theatre are spelt out in the 1597 Petition by the Lord Mayor and Aldermen of London to have the playhouses 'plucked down', which is worth quoting in detail:

Firstly, they corrupt youth, containing nothing but unchaste matters and ungodly practices which impress the very quality and corruption of manners which they represent, contrary to the rules and art prescribed for them even among the heathen, who used them seldom and at set times and not all the year long.

Secondly, they are the ordinary places for vagrant persons, masterless men, thieves, horse-stealers, whoremongers, cozeners, connycatchers, contrivers of treason and other dangerous persons to meet together and to make their matches, which cannot be prevented when discovered by the governors of the City, for that they are out of the City's jurisdiction.

Thirdly, they maintain idleness in persons with no vocation and draw prentices and other servants from their ordinary work, and all sorts from resort to sermons and other Christian exercises, to the great hindrance of trades and profanation of religion.

Fourthly, in time of sickness many having sores and yet not heartsick take occasion to walk abroad and hear a play, whereby others are infected and themselves also many times miscarry.

The association made at the beginning of the Petition between the theatre and 'nothing' was a common one. The City authorities claim that playhouses contain 'nothing but unchaste matters and ungodly practices', which was equivalent to saying that it contained nothing but nothing. The Petition ends with specific instructions for the demolition of these temples of nothingness:

... that the Curtain and Theatre in Shoreditch and the playhouses on the Bankside shall be plucked down, and present order taken that no plays be used in any public place within three miles of the City till Allhallow tide. Likewise the magistrates shall send for the owners of the playhouses and enjoin them to pluck down quite the stages, galleries and rooms and so to deface them that they may not again be employed to such use.

The final reference to the need to 'deface' the playhouses confirms other accounts which draw attention to colourful and ostentatious exterior decorations. Such gaudy flamboyance, a real case of nothing pretending to be something, caused particular offence to the City authorities. Petitions against the theatre were invariably couched in moralistic terms. Self-interest was nevertheless an important reason for such attacks: the preachers had to compete with the theatres for audiences and aldermen usually had carefully invested interests in promoting industry.

A critical eye was also turned on the actors as well as their audiences. It was often held that they were social nobodies, or nothings, to be classed with the 'vagrant persons' and others who haunted the theatres, and nightmares, of Elizabethan society. To make matters worse, it was all too common on stage for the toe of the peasant actor to be inside the shoe of the courtier. That may have been show business, but for some it offered a disturbing vision of a world, or body politic, turned upside down. Such extreme responses to the theatre were undermined by its increasing professionalization during the late Elizabethan and early Jacobean periods. It became merely reactionary to liken the new breed of actors – with their noble patrons, smart liveries, shrewd investments and even personal coats of arms – to common players.

A subt'er form of hostility nevertheless still persisted, often but not exclusively associated with forms of Puritanism. The actor was all things to all people because he could be all people. This meant that his own personality was at best fluid and flexible, at worst nothing. Paradoxically, everything was being played by nothing. The theatres, as the 1597 Petition indicates, were a threat because they lay outside 'the City's jurisdiction'. The actors were a threat because they lay outside a moral jurisdiction based upon patience, perseverance and, above all, constancy. It was not not just a case of a man playing far too many parts in his life. The convention of using boy actors, or 'playboys', to act the woman's part offered the possibility of sexual as well as social confusion and anarchy. John Rainoldes, a Puritan theologian and Oxford academic, was quick to point out some of the dire consequences of this practice in a collection of pamphlets published under the title of *The Overthrow of Stage Plays* (1599): 'the putting of womens attire upon men may kindle sparkes of lust in uncleane affections'. Forms of transvestitism threatened to drag decent people into the abyss.

The actor's personality, such as it was, became symbolized by outward appearances in general and extravagant clothes in particular. These clothes, to add insult to injury, were often either hand-downs or purchases from deceased gentlefolk. Every society has its unwritten laws about what its members ought to wear. Those who themselves lack style often attempt to write up these laws. Elizabethan society produced more than its fair share of such handbooks ostensibly designed to make the upwardly mobile feel more comfortable. Yet these manuals often went against the written and official laws governing style or 'apparel'. Fears that the statutes which laid down who could wear what were being neglected led to two Royal Proclamations, in 1588 and 1597, on Enforcing Statutes and Proclamations of Apparel. The 1588 Proclamation was concerned to prevent 'inordinate excess in apparel' leading to 'the confusion of degrees of all estates'. Such confusion heralded the triumph of nothing over something. Clothes could prevent such anarchy if they were used to denote rank or degree: peasants and courtiers were required by law to dress as such. The 1597 Proclamation reiterated the same conservative message:

None shall wear in his apparel cloth of gold or silver tissued, silk of color purple under the degree of an earl, except Knights of the Garter in their purple mantles only ... None shall wear spurs, swords, rapiers, daggers, skeans, woodknives, or hangers, buckles of girdles gilt, silvered, or damasked, except knights and barons' sons and others of high degree or place, and gentlemen in ordinary office attendant upon the Queen's majesty's person, which gentlemen so attendant may wear all the premises saving gilt, silvered, or damasked spurs.

Women's clothes came in for the same close scrutiny:

None shall wear any velvet, tufted taffeta, satin, or any gold or silver in their petticoats, except wives of barons, knights of the order, or councilors; ladies and gentlewomen of the privy chamber and bed chamber; and the maidens of honor ... No person under the degrees above specified shall wear any guard or welt of silk upon any petticoat, cloak, or safeguard.

The argument had an important economic dimension since extravagant apparel was often imported from Europe. The actor's love for such apparel was subversive at a more general level since it flouted these written laws which tried to enforce the rule that appearance should proclaim reality. Ultimately, the theatre inverted these laws by making appearance the only reality.

The various critiques of the theatre during the Elizabethan period argued, often quite precisely, that it was dangerous because it represented much ado about nothing. It may not be too fanciful to imagine less ideologically committed members of Shakespeare's audiences dismissing particular plays or performances as being much ado about nothing, or rubbish. This time Shakespeare beats them all to it. Their last words become his first words or title. Their negative responses to theatricality provide the starting point for his celebration of it. He takes a familiar, almost clichéd, criticism of the theatre and throws it back triumphantly at his solemn opponents. This reading of the title explains, in so far as such things can be explained, why the play itself draws such explicit attention to its own theatricality and artificiality. As suggested, it consists of plays within plays within plays, which are often very self-consciously watched by an on-stage audience as well as by the theatre one. The main themes concern the deceptive nature of appearances and the power of illusions. At one level, such an open display of and revelling in theatricality can be seen in terms of festive celebration. There may, however, be a more serious point. The critics argued that the theatre was nothing because it preferred show to substance, spectacle to meaning and parts to personality. The assumption was that real life and theatrical life were radically different. Yet Shakespeare and others frequently challenged such crude categorizations by drawing attention to the 'stage-play world' which existed beyond the theatres. To take just one example, Macbeth's speech after he has received the report of Lady Macbeth's death offers a pessimistic variation on this *theatrum mundi* theme:

> *Life's but a walking shadow; a poor player*
> *That struts and frets his hour upon the stage*
> *And then is heard no more. It is a tale*
> *Told by an idiot, full of sound and fury,*
> *Signifying nothing.*

(V. v. 24–8)

Macbeth sees both life and the theatre as representing much ado about nothing. Yet, if the theatre makes much ado, or great display, of its nothingness, then it might signify something. Theatrical pageants may be insubstantial ones but, paradoxically, they become more substantial through the self-conscious exhibition of limitations. *Much Ado*'s revelation of artifice through revelling in it transforms nothing into something of great moment or much ado.

The Elizabethans sometimes used the phrase 'much ado' to mean a lot of difficulty or bother. It was also used just to mean a lot of action in general. Both meanings fit the themes of the play. Comedy is often defined by its excessive concentration on excess. A very familiar comic device is to take a particular situation and reduce it to absurdity through constant repetition. The title of *Much Ado About Nothing* can be read as both a dirty joke and a complicated philosophical riddle. It can also be seen as a playful polemic against those who literally tried to put down the theatre in the 1590s. At a more general level, it forecasts a 'comic climate' of exuberance and excess. The sheer quantity of the plays and deceptions which form the structure of *Much Ado* raises the playful problem of what is in excess of excess.

3 Shakespeare's Sources

Introduction

It was standard practice for Elizabethan students at schools and universities to imitate passages from classical authors. Imitation was seen as an art rather than a suspect craft. It encouraged invention for the object was not just to retell a 'mouldy tale' but to reinterpret it. The basic theme was introduced so that variations could be played upon it. At a more general level, Renaissance education was based upon what has been called the 'rhetorical ideal of life'. This meant that there was a strong emphasis, in 'composition' exercises as well as 'delivery' ones, on eloquence. Original thought or sincere conviction are highly valued today. The Elizabethans were more interested in developing fluent and effective expression.

There are, of course, important differences between the imitation of short, well-known passages from Classical authors and the use of more contemporary material as the basis for stage plays. Yet, fundamentally, the two activities were judged according to the same general standards. Elizabethan audiences did not expect original plots or parts. If they defined originality at all, it was in terms of the playwright's ability to rearrange and reinterpret existing materials. Thus, discussions of Shakespeare's sources which hint darkly at plagiarism are in danger of missing the point. Shakespeare certainly sailed pretty close to the wind on occasions, for instance with his heavy reliance on Thomas Lodge's prose romance *Rosalynde* (1590) for the plot of *As You Like It*. Yet, in general terms, his use of sources was perfectly in keeping with both current theory and practice.

Ariosto

Early Italian Renaissance literature provided Shakespeare with the sources for *Much Ado*. Some critics suggest that his starting point was Ludovico Ariosto's *Orlando Furioso* (1516), perhaps not in the original Italian but rather in one of its subsequent English versions or variations. Sir John Harington's 1591 translation is probably the strongest candidate. A play based around Ariosto's tale of Ariodante and Genevra was performed at Court at the beginning of 1583 by boys from Merchant Taylor's School, although the text has not survived. There has been some speculation about whether it might have been based on Peter Beverley's poem *Ariodante and Jenevra* (1566). Edmund Spenser's *The Faerie Queene* (1596) also contains a poetic variation of the Ariodante and Genevra story.

Book Five of *Orlando Furioso* deals with the triangular relationship between Genevra, who is the King of Scotland's daughter, and her two lovers, Ariodante and Polynesso. Ariodante is a 'comely Italian knight' whose love for Genevra is genuine. Polynesso, the Duke of Alban, has a more mercenary attitude towards her as he wants to marry her to further his own dynastic ambitions within Scotland. It is also possible that his 'good friendship' with Ariodante leads him into rivalry almost for its own sake. Genevra's love for Ariodante remains constant, so Polynesso fashions a plot to dishonour her and discredit his rival. He has been enjoying the 'fruites of loves delight' with Genevra's maid, Dalinda, for some time. He has even tried to use her as a stepping stone to her mistress. He now suggests that the only cure for his infatuation with Genevra is for Dalinda to pretend to be her mistress. She agrees to come to her mistress's window at night dressed like her and to let Polynesso climb in. Dalinda does not know that this play is being acted out for the benefit of Ariodante and his brother Luciano, who are watching from the garden. The narrative structure is such that these events form part of Dalinda's confession to the chivalrous knight, Renaldo:

> *I that his comming willingly did wayt,*
> *And he once come thought nothing went amisse,*
> *Embrac't him kindly at the first receyt,*
> *His lips, his cheeks, and all his face did kisse,*
> *And he the more to colour his deceyt,*
> *Used me kinder than he had ere this.*
> *This sight much care to* Ariodante *brought*
> *Thinking* Genevra *with the Duke was nought.*

In this context, 'nought' means naughty or immoral. Ariodante disappears from the scene and is presumed to have drowned himself. His brother, Luciano, proclaims Genevra's guilt. According to the 'harsh' Scottish law, she will be burnt at the stake unless somebody comes forward to proclaim her innocence, which would involve challenging the lecherous, treacherous Polynesso to mortal combat. To simplify the complicated ending, this is exactly what Renaldo does, after he has rescued Dalinda from Polynesso's henchmen and heard her confession. Polynesso is mortally wounded in the combat and confesses to his crimes. Ariodante is not dead but has also come, in disguise, to challenge Polynesso. Dalinda's relationship with Polynesso shows how love leads to deception. Genevra's relationship with Ariodante shows how love leads to a period of suffering. Renaldo proves that Fortune can be kind as well as cruel.

The deception of Ariodante is broadly similar to that practised upon Claudio in *Much Ado*. The significant difference is that, whereas in *Orlando Furioso* a rival lover stages the play, in *Much Ado* Don John has no romantic intentions towards Hero. He and Polynesso both try to 'colour' or mask their deceit, but they act from different motives. The Ariosto version also differs from Shakespeare's as far as the actions of the deceived lover, the Claudio figure, are concerned. It is Ariodante rather than Genevra who is presumed dead. It is Luciano rather than Ariodante who publicly shames Genevra. The locations are also miles apart. Shakespeare sets his scene in Messina in Sicily, whereas Ariosto's story takes place in Scotland. An adaptation was not, however, expected to be a faithful copy.

Bandello

Critics who are not convinced about the influence of Ariosto on *Much Ado* tend to turn their attention to Matteo Bandello instead. Bandello is a curiously neglected figure: curious because, at the very least, he provided a model for two of the most famous Renaissance plays, *Romeo and Juliet* and *The Duchess of Malfi*. The stories which provided the initial inspiration for Shakespeare and John Webster were translated by William Painter for his *The Palace of Pleasure* (1566 and 1567). Bandello was also a significant influence on the development of the Elizabethan prose romance, despite the fact that his work did not reach the literary market in its original form. English translators and adaptors tended themselves to be working from translations and adaptations, notably by French writers such as Pierre Boaistuau and François de Belleforrest. These writers often tried to improve Bandello by playing down his emphasis on sensuality in favour of sentimentality. It is not known which version Shakespeare might have consulted, although the conjecture must be that, like the majority of his contemporaries, he worked at one or quite possibly two stages removed from the originals.

The story which seems to lie behind *Much Ado* is the twenty-second one from *La Prima Parte de le Novelle del Bandello* (1554). Bandello, like Shakespeare, sets his scene in Messina. He is more precise, however, with the historical setting. His narrative begins immediately after the notorious Sicilian Vespers of 1282. The Sicilians expelled their French rulers and invited King Pedro of Aragon to become their new monarch. Bandello's narrative starts with a King Piero in control of the island, but worried about the possibility of a counter-attack from Naples. He therefore decides to move his base from Palermo to Messina. His knights carry on with their victory celebrations, which literally become a movable feast. Sir Timbreo di Cardona falls in love with Fenicia, who is the daughter of Lionato de Lionati. Although Lionato is described as 'a nobleman of Messina' whose 'lineage . . . was ancient and noble and of great reputation', he is not in the same league as grandees such as Sir Timbreo. His family is obviously coming down in the world as his income is only that of a 'private gentleman'. Timbreo and Fenicia nevertheless conduct a ritualistic public courtship. The knight's motives are far from honourable ones:

The gentleman grew warmer every day and the more he gazed on her the more he felt his desire to burn, and, the fire increasing in his heart so much that he felt himself consumed with love for the beautiful maiden, he determined he must have her at any cost.

He wants to seduce Fenicia rather than marry her. Fenicia cools down her warm knight by ignoring his love letters. He realizes that the wicked way is not getting him anywhere fast and so, after much 'inner debate' about whether he would be 'demeaning himself' by such a marriage, decides to do the decent thing. He therefore asks a friend of his to play the part of matchmaker with Lionato, who is ever so pleased that this grand knight should 'condescend to ally himself to him'. The course of true love never did run quite as smoothly as this or, as the narrator puts it, 'Fortune, which never ceases to work against the wellbeing of mankind, found a novel means of stopping the marriage.'

Fortune's tool is a local suitor, Sir Girondo Olerio Valenziano, who hardly seems to fall into the category of 'novel means'. He was also warmed up by the sight of Fenicia and was in fact in 'such a frenzy of amorous desire that he lost all sense of reason'. He is still able to fashion a plot to dishonour Fenicia. He persuades an acquaintance of his to tell Timbreo that the lady plays him false. This ungallant gallant is described as 'a young courtier, a fellow of little upbringing, more pleased with evil than with good'. He tells Timbreo that Fenicia already has a lover who comes around 'twice or three times a week to sleep with her and enjoy her love'. He suggests that Timbreo ought to hide in some ruins near Lionato's garden and watch these proceedings for himself. The poor knight is himself a bit of a ruin when he takes up his position:

it seemed to him impossible that Fenicia would have yielded herself to another. Then he said to himself that young girls are changeable, light, unstable, disdainful and eager for new things; and so, now excusing her, now accusing her, he waited tensely for any sign of movement.

The sight, and smell, of a 'perfumed gallant' mounting a ladder up to

Fenicia's window confirms all his worst suspicions. This particular gallant is in fact one of Girondo's servants, who has been 'decked out' to play the part. He presumably hopes to be able to scale a few rungs on the social ladder by 'simulating' the role of lover to oblige his master.

Timbreo is now warmed up with jealousy rather than with desire. He still behaves rationally and sends his go-between round to Lionato's house to break off the engagement:

To you Fenicia he says that the love which he bore you did not deserve the bitter reward you have given him, and that you should find yourself another husband, just as you have already found yourself another lover; or rather indeed you should take the man to whom you have given your virginity. Sir Timbreo does not intend to have anything more to do with you, since you will make anyone who marries you a Lord of Corneto.

Lionato suspects that all this stuff about Corneto, or cuckoldry, is nonsense and that Timbreo is just looking for an excuse to break off the engagement. Fenicia takes it more seriously and lets 'herself sink down like a dead woman'. She rouses herself to deliver a conventional 'death is better than dishonour' speech and then falls back into a trance. Arrangements are made for her funeral but, once again, she rises from the dead. Lionato decides to pack her off to the country to stay with his brother, Girolano, so that 'he might marry her off in two or three years under another name'. With this, rather than thoughts of shaming Timbreo in mind, he orders her funeral to go ahead without her. Timbreo is greatly moved by the whole affair and experiences 'great sorrow and a heartstirring such as he would never have thought possible'. Girondo is shocked into a confession. The sorrowful Timbreo appears to be just as wounded by his friend's betrayal as he is by Fenicia's supposed death. He extols the noble virtues of male friendship over the naughty vices of heterosexual desire:

you ought to have revealed to me your love, since you knew of my love for her and I did not know of yours. For then I should have relinquished my amorous enterprise to you before asking her father for her hand, and, as magnanimous and generous spirits are accustomed to do, in overcoming myself I should have preferred our friendship to my desire ...

Once he thinks that he knows the full facts Timbreo, magnanimous as ever, takes Girondo along to Lionato's house so that they can get everything off their chests. The old man is, however, playing his cards close to *his* chest. He has no difficulty in getting the penitent Timbreo to promise that when you wish to marry you will be so good as to let me know, and that if I offer you a lady who pleases you you will take her.

A year later, he invites Timbreo to go into the country to meet just such a lady, who goes under the name of Lucilla. The knight is 'wonderfully taken with her at first sight' so a wedding ceremony is speedily performed. The groom is asked during the wedding feast whether he has ever been married before and he and Girondo seem almost grateful to tumble out their confessions again. This time they make them in front of Fenicia herself for she and Lucilla are one and the same. No masks are necessary to conceal her identity up to this point since a year in the country air has apparently changed her a good deal. Fortune has at last stopped plotting against the young lovers and they head back to Messina for a lavish reception laid on by King Piero. They are accompanied by Girondo and his new bride, who is Fenicia's young cousin Belfoire. The narrator adds that

both of them enjoyed their ladies henceforth for a long time, living in the greatest peace, often recalling to each other with pleasure the misadventures of the fair Fenicia.

Fortune has failed to undermine the smug well-being of this particular male friendship.

Bandello's novella, often referred to in shorthand as *Timbreo and Fenicia*, seems closer to the structure of *Much Ado* than Ariosto's tale of Ariodante and Genevra does. The main points of comparison between Bandello's version and Shakespeare's may be listed as follows. First, and perhaps foremost, they both have a Sicilian setting. Secondly, there are similarities between some of the names. Bandello's Piero and Lionato are close to Shakespeare's Pedro and Leonato. Thirdly, the matchmaking is undertaken by go-betweens in both versions, although Shakespeare exploits the dramatic potential of the situation much more than Bandello does. Fourthly, Timbreo and Claudio are both deceived by a similar kind of 'window trick'. Shakespeare does not, however, include a dramatization of this incident. Elizabethan stages were equipped with a gallery, which would have been the obvious location for such a scene, although evidence suggests it was primarily used for occasional action and stage business rather than for lengthy or important parts of a play. The omission is anyway perfectly in keeping with *Much Ado*'s stress on the role of hearsay and slander. Fifthly, Fenicia and Hero are both presumed to be dead and, when they recover, it is still announced that they are dead. Finally, there are broad similarities between the resolutions of the two versions. Timbreo and Fenicia, Claudio and Hero marry in an atmosphere of forgiveness and reconciliation. More specifically, Timbreo and Claudio both agree at short notice to a marriage with a close friend or relative of their 'dead' bride.

Differences are often more interesting than similarities when considering Shakespeare's use of sources. Bandello's version highlights tensions within Sicilian society between the Spanish grandees and the native gentry at a specific historical moment. As indicated, *Much Ado* does not have such a precise historical setting. Social distinctions are also flattened out, although perhaps not so much as is generally believed. Don Pedro is obviously at the top of the play's social pyramid and Leonato thus asks him to lead the procession into the Governor's house:

LEONATO   *Please it your grace lead on?*
DON PEDRO *Your hand, Leonato; we will go together.*

(I. i. 150–51)

Don Pedro's gesture, dramatically effective in its own right but also part of a pattern of handing and unhanding throughout the play, should not be taken to imply equality between the two men. It signals, rather, Don Pedro's wish for a temporary suspension of rigid social etiquette during the festivities that are to follow the end of the war. These festivities are disrupted by Claudio's rejection of Hero and so is this temporary equality. Don Pedro, Don John and Claudio all stand on their dignity during the denunciation scene, a fact which does not escape Beatrice's attention. She is no longer able to put her faith in princes. One of these princes, Don John, uses the need to preserve social distinction as his professed motive during his first plot against Claudio. *Much Ado* therefore retains some of Bandello's emphasis on class conflict, without making it a focal point.

The denunciation is one of Shakespeare's additions to the story, as indeed is Claudio's repentance at Hero's tomb. Both scenes effectively dramatize Claudio's limitations. Fenicia and Hero are similar kinds of heroine, both being young, modest and essentially passive. Yet Timbreo and Claudio have different approaches to love and marriage. Timbreo only considers marriage after his heated attempts at seduction have proved to be much ado about nothing. Claudio, on the other hand, is interested in marriage from the very start. He grows very heated during the denunciation scene when Leonato thinks that he might be confessing to sleeping with Hero between the betrothal and the wedding. Such a practice, quite common in Elizabethan England, was not completely condoned by the Church but was seen as being mildly irregular rather than blatantly illegal. There is, indeed, nobody quite like Claudio in the other versions of the story. One critic, working on the Ariosto tradition, suggests that

Shakespeare edited out the more conventional lover as *Much Ado* was designed to raise specific questions about arranged marriages. Claudio's marriage is certainly arranged for him by Don Pedro, although the original impetus behind it comes from Claudio himself. Another problem with this interpretation is that the Elizabethans would not have regarded the arranged marriage as a separate and easily identifiable category. The vast majority of marriages were arranged ones and the vast majority of people accepted the arrangement. This is not to say that some of Shakespeare's plays, for instance *The Taming of the Shrew* and *The Merry Wives of Windsor*, do not question extreme versions of this orthodoxy. It is to suggest, rather, that the evidence is not strong enough to claim that the arranged marriage *per se* is one of the central themes of *Much Ado*. Claudio's response to Hero takes romantic as well as apparently mercenary forms, which indicates that arranged marriages do not necessarily preclude love. The sources draw attention to the problem of Claudio, but they do not solve it.

Perhaps the most significant difference between Shakespeare's and Bandello's versions concerns the absence of the Girondo character. Shakespeare retains the emphasis on male friendship by building up the relationship between Pedro and Claudio, but Hero is not slandered by a rival lover. This is done by Don John, who has no romantic feelings towards her – or anybody else for that matter. This may be his motive. He despises marriage and all it stands for and is thus prepared to fashion plots against it. The substitution of these anti-romantic motives for the ones associated with the jilted Girondo allows Shakespeare, once again, to concentrate on a broader representation of the kind of deception built on hearsay and rumour. If, as will be argued later, Don John is seen as a comic villain, then his inclusion at the expense of Girondo obviously enhances the play's comedy.

As will be apparent, the debate over the sources for *Much Ado* is confined almost exclusively to the Claudio–Hero plot. Ariosto, Bandello and others do not seem to be much help when it comes to the parts of Don John, Beatrice and Benedick, and Dogberry and the Watch. The conventional explanation is that although Claudio, Hero, Leonato and Don Pedro have at least their origins in Italian literature, these other parts are very much Shakespeare's own 'creations'. They are, however, all very recognizable stage-types, in some cases with their origins in Classical Roman comedy: Dogberry the bumbling official, Benedick the selfish bachelor, Beatrice the disdainful lady and Don John the comic villain. Indeed, it is entirely appropriate for such stage-types to be parts in a play which takes delight in displaying its own heightened theatricality. The real source for *Much Ado* is the theatre. Although the terminology is clumsy, it would be safer to argue that Shakespeare develops these parts creatively rather than creating them.

Castiglione

There have been attempts to provide Beatrice and Benedick with a more specifically Renaissance pedigree. The most interesting one is the suggestion that they may be rather distant relations of Lady Emilia Pia and Gaspare Pallavicino, two characters from Baldesar Castiglione's influential *The Book of the Courtier* (1528). The courtiers at Urbino are certainly impressed by Emilia's wit:

a lady gifted with such a lively wit and judgement ... that she seemed to be the mistress of all and to endow everyone else with her own discernment and goodness.

The text itself provides little justification for such high praise. Emilia is occasionally stung into a sharp one-liner by Gaspare's remarks on women:

And signor Gaspare remarked with a smile: 'Now you cannot complain that the signor Magnifico has not formed a truly excellent Court lady; and from now on, if any such lady be discovered, I declare that she deserves to be regarded as the equal of the courtier.' Signora Emilia retorted: 'I will guarantee to discover her, if you will find the courtier.'

As Gaspare is occasionally held to be 'anti-feminist', it may be important to stress that he is primarily concerned to argue against the kind of idealization of women associated with Petrarchan poetry. Lady Emilia, for the most part, seems quite content to play the role of a talk-show hostess who paces and umpires the discussions according to the rules. This means, certainly on the first three nights, making sure that 'tiresome' or philosophical points are not allowed to bore this charmed and charming circle of courtiers. She occasionally bends the rules by calling on a completely inappropriate speaker for a particular topic. Her pert wit is nevertheless different from Beatrice's broader and more aggressive brand. If Beatrice has to have a literary pedigree, then Shakespeare himself provided her with one in Kate from *The Taming of the Shrew*.

   Lady Emilia's role in the conversations which form *The Courtier* can be related to *Much Ado* more profitably at a general level. The Court at Urbino is presided over by Duchess Elizabetta Gonzaga. All the conversations take place in her room after dinner. Her own interventions tend to be confined to letting everybody know when it is time to leave. She does not, however, need to say anything because she is quite obviously the candle that attracts all the courtly moths. They are trying to impress her as much as themselves. Lady Emilia, on the other hand, has to gain attention through her attempts at wit. Both women are fulfilling different 'domestic' functions: Elizabetta is an adornment to be admired, whereas Emilia provides organization and light relief. This is a general form of stereotyping and as such parallels the roles that Hero and Beatrice are expected to play in *Much Ado*. The silent Hero is the object of the admiring gaze and praise, whereas the talkative Beatrice has to capture attention through her wit. The differences are that both Hero and Beatrice are younger than their counterparts in *The Courtier* and are also still to be married. *The Courtier* provides an interesting context for the study of *Much Ado*, but should not be taken as a specific source for it.

Conclusions

A study of Shakespeare's possible sources can be a useful critical exercise, particularly for the English and Roman history plays. It is not, however, the most rewarding way of approaching *Much Ado*. The influence of Italian literature is reasonably clear. It still remains to be established whether, more precisely, *Much Ado* can be called an Italianate play. Even bearing in mind the freedom and licence which Renaissance adaptors brought to their work, it seems likely that Bandello's version was the one which Shakespeare used. The Sicilian setting for *Much Ado* is probably the most convincing evidence for this necessarily tentative judgement. Bandello's story has a number of main themes: class conflict, the role of Fortune and the rival claims of male friendship and marriage. These themes, particularly the last one, certainly form a part of *Much Ado*. Yet the play is more concerned to explore the power and persistence of illusions. Some of the differences between Bandello's story and Shakespeare's play can be seen as attempts to heighten the theatricality of Messinese society, for instance the inclusion of a denunciation scene. Others point in the direction of an increased emphasis on hearsay and rumour, for instance the absence of a rival lover in *Much Ado*. Heightened theatricality, and the hearsay upon which it is often based, strengthen this central concern with illusion. A study of the sources can pose important questions, for instance about Claudio's relationship with Hero, but the answers have to be found elsewhere.

4 Some Representations of Italy and Spain

Introduction

Italy was larger than life and twice the size for Elizabethan and Jacobean theatre audiences. It has been estimated that at least one third of the plays performed between 1549 and 1640 had either Italian sources or locations. In most cases it was both. As has just been shown, *Much Ado* clearly falls into this broad category. It has been suggested, more specifically, that the play is Shakespeare's most Italian, or Italianate. At first such an argument is difficult to follow. In what respects, for instance, is *Much Ado* any more Italianate than, say, *Romeo and Juliet* or *Othello*? The suspicion must be that it is given this label because critics feel that there is precious little else to say about it. The point can be treated more sympathetically. *Much Ado* illustrates the cultural and political mix of Renaissance Italy better than many other plays. The scene may be set exclusively in Messina but the parts represent, if not quite a league of nations, then at least a wide variety of backgrounds and allegiances. Don Pedro and Don John represent the territorial and cultural power of the Hapsburgs. Claudio is a young Florentine, whereas Benedick is a gentleman from Padua. It probably has to be assumed that, at the general level of prejudice, Elizabethan audiences were attuned to differences between these two cities in much the same way as modern ones can spot variations between Denver and Dallas. Conrade and Borachio are of unspecified origin, although their actions suggest that they would be quite at home in a sink of depravity like Venice. The play also introduces native Sicilians such as Leonato, Hero and Beatrice.

There is, then, a case for seeing *Much Ado* as an Italianate play. It has to be remembered, however, that for Shakespeare's audiences Italianate was a pejorative term. It is thus perfectly possible for *Much Ado* to be both an Italianate play and an intensely English or chauvinistic one. The chauvinism of a play like *Henry V* is difficult to explain away, but there has been a certain amount of critical special pleading to try to exempt Shakespeare's Italian plays from such a charge. It is sometimes claimed that, whilst his contemporary dramatists were content to wallow in blood-and-thunder interpretations of Italian life, he came closer to representing the kind of idyllic version associated with Ariosto and Castiglione. According to such an interpretation, Shakespeare can still be seen as a humanist even though his contemporaries were little better than

39

thriller-writers. In other words, Shakespeare has to share the same prejudices as his critics. It is more likely, however, that he had the same prejudices as his contemporaries.

Elizabethan and Jacobean dramatists emphasized the steamy, seamy side of Italian life. This is what their audiences loved to hate. Vice has always been better box office than virtue. *Romeo and Juliet*, despite later attempts to sentimentalize it, offers a 'drugs and damnation', 'poison and passion' interpretation of Italian life. Juliet's mother may be rather ineffectual, but she at least knows the right lines:

> *We will have vengeance for it, fear thou not.*
> *Then weep no more. I'll send to one in Mantua,*
> *Where that same banished runagate doth live,*
> *Shall give him such an unaccostumed dram*
> *That he shall soon keep Tybalt company.*
> *And then I hope thou wilt be satisfied.*
>
> (III. v. 87–92)

The play's revenge theme is accompanied by familiar Italianate parts and props: swaggering swordsmen, dubious friars, stifling vaults and festering shrouds. Italy excited the theatrical imagination not just because it provided an ideal location for depravity. Its appeal lay in a particular combination of the splendid and the sordid. Dramatists like John Webster were often content to convey this splendour through references to magnificent palaces and fine clothes. Shakespeare was more interested in relationships between noble ideals and sordid realities: the Italians may grovel in the mud but they are also reaching for the sky. This double vision controls *The Tempest*. Prospero, the great Renaissance magus, allows himself to become the victim of city-state politics and is expelled from Milan by Antonio and the King of Naples. Italian life is therefore represented as a mixture of sophistication and cunning, high learning and low morality. Such an interpretation is itself more sophisticated than those which merely emphasized cunning and intrigue, but is nevertheless hardly an idyllic one.

There were more prosaic reasons for the popularity of Italian themes and locations. Dramatists were able to escape the unwelcome attentions of the Master of the Revels, who acted as an official censor, if their scene was set in Italy. Ben Jonson found himself in prison on a couple of occasions for writing satires that were a little too close to home. The Lord Chamberlain's Men were examined by the Privy Council about their unwise decision to stage *Richard II*, complete with the deposition scene, on the eve of the Earl of Essex's rebellion in 1601. Literally and metaphorically, it was easier to get away with murder when it took place in Italy. A parody of an Italian court was fair game, whereas one of the Elizabethan Court itself was foul treason. Given the Italianate influences on Elizabethan high society in the 1590s, stage representations of Italy could fulfil two separate functions. They could reinforce chauvinistic prejudices, whilst at the same time they could also be satirizing contemporary English values.

The polarity between humanism and sensationalism is rather a misleading one. Although modern interpretations of the Italian Renaissance deal extensively with Florentine civilization, Shakespeare's contemporaries were not well informed about such cultural achievements. They knew more about Florentine politics than painting. Indeed, English travellers to Italy in the sixteenth century paid little attention to painting. Florence therefore served as a more general location for Italianate manners and morals. Bertram, in *All's Well That Ends Well*, leaves 'the dark house and the detested wife' (II. iii. 290) in France and escapes to Florence. He is after excitement rather than knowledge. Florence, in contrast to the decaying French Court, is young and vigorous. It offers plenty of action as a result of city-state feuds. Bertram also hopes to be able to combine this with a bit of lust on the side. Shakespeare's audiences, some of whom may have made their own escape from 'the dark house and the detested wife', expected their theatrical trip to Florence to show fast living rather than high learning.

The Florentine Michael Cassio, in *Othello*, conforms to and therefore confirms English stereotypes of the Italians. Iago represents him as a gentlemanly officer who knows more about the show of war than its substance. He is, in this respect, like Count Malateste in *The Duchess of Malfi*. Iago draws particular attention to Cassio's rhetoric: 'Mere prattle without practice' (I. l. 25). Italians were quite frequently referred to as 'prattlers' in pamphlets from the 1590s and 1600s. Foreigners, usually called either 'strangers' or 'aliens', were not the flavour of these particular decades. Iago, trying to prejudice both Roderigo and the audience against Cassio, notices how 'prattle' is, in reality, the basis of his courtiership as well as his soldiership. Cassio greets Desdemona when she arrives in Cyprus with extravagant rhetorical gestures. These are accompanied by physical ones, such as kneeling before her and then taking her hand. He then makes a 'bold show of courtesy' (II. i. 99) by greeting Emilia with a kiss. These flamboyant performances in the role of the Italian courtier would have prejudiced Jacobean audiences against him, regardless of whether Iago was there to cue such a reaction. Iago's commentary indicates that Cassio plays the part to the hilt:

He takes her by the palm. Ay, well said, whisper. With as little a web as this will I ensnare as great a fly as Cassio. Ay, smile upon her, do. I will gyve thee in thine own courtship. You say true, 'tis so indeed. If such tricks as these strip you out of your lieutenantry, it had been better you had not kissed your three fingers so oft, which now again you are most apt to play the sir in.

(II. i. 164–71)

Other evidence confirms that Italians on the Elizabethan and Jacobean stage were instantly recognizable by such mannerisms as hand-kissing, or what might be described today as blowing kisses. These gestures confirmed a view of courtesy or courtiership which saw it as being either effeminate or narcissistic. Despite Cassio's patronizing relationship with Bianca, Iago's charge that he is 'almost damned in a fair wife' (I. i. 21) is one that sticks. Iago also manipulates the audience against him by praising the Englishman's alcoholic capacity just before he exits pursued by a hangover and Roderigo. The Italians themselves often contrasted their own temperance or restraint with the Englishman's boorish intemperance. The point was frequently made by John Florio, the author of two successful 'teach yourself Italian' manuals, *First Fruits* (1578) and *Second Fruits* (1591). Iago cunningly reverses the compliment. Such cunning meant that he himself conformed to another Italian stereotype. Cassio, the courtier, is concerned with show and reputation whereas Iago, the Machiavellian villain, manipulates both outward appearances and other people's concern for them. Even such a cursory glance at *Othello* indicates that Shakespeare's Italy was far from idyllic. *Othello* plays tragic variations on some of the comic themes of *Much Ado*. Don John, the aspiring Machiavellian villain, is a joke. Don Pedro and Claudio take Cassio's brand of courtiership to comic extremes. Italianate manners and mannerisms are treated chauvinistically rather than respectfully.

In general, Elizabethan and Jacobean audiences liked to laugh at Italian courtiers and hiss Italian villains. Italy was rarely if ever presented in purely humanistic terms. Its inhabitants were seen as being hot, volatile, temperamental, vain and cunning. Spiritual as well as physical danger was usually in the air since, as the home of Popery, Italy was a potential threat to all Protestants. The potent theatrical combination of religious cloaks, political daggers and courtly finery created an attraction and repulsion for the Italianate. Italy itself represented a poisoned fountain, at which addicted theatre audiences queued up to try to slake an unquenchable thirst for the exotic, exciting and entertaining. Shakespeare may not have written Italianate 'nasties' in the style of Webster, but is nevertheless closer to the prejudices of his contemporaries than his humanistic admirers are prepared to admit.

Castiglione again

Castiglione's *The Courtier* was available to Shakespeare and his audiences in Sir Thomas Hoby's 1561 translation. The perspective was essentially an idealistic and nostalgic one. Instead of providing the more conventional manual which told aspiring courtiers how to dress and behave, Castiglione was more concerned to evoke the mood and atmosphere of the glory that was Urbino. The conversations appear to be almost timeless, but this is to give them permanence in a transitory world. The narrator comments at the beginning of the Fourth Book on the way in which death was to disrupt this courtly circle. The narration is retrospective and tinged with regret. By contrast, Shakespeare's representation of courtly life in *Much Ado* is mediated by irreverence and humour rather than by this kind of affectionate recall. Shakespeare and Castiglione nevertheless share at least two common themes, despite these fundamental differences in perspective. Castiglione believed that the courtier needed to be an actor, albeit rather an understated one. Conversation is an art which has to be cultivated. It is shown, particularly in the first three books, to be an eloquent, rhetorical, essentially theatrical exercise in which fluency is more important than sincerity. All the courtiers are given the 'privilege of contradiction', which means that particular points of view have to be argued against to maintain the symmetry, or pattern, of the argument. Flexibility is more important than conviction. The courtier is also advised to tailor his conversational performances to suit his particular audiences. A private conversation with a prince calls for different skills from those required to impress during an after-dinner conversation in mixed company. Courtiership, like acting, is a work of art in itself. Castiglione implies, however, that this necessary artifice ought to be unaffected and understated. The courtier is expected to wear a number of masks in order to perform well in the stylized society, but the most important one is the mask that covers this masking. One commentator suggests that *The Courtier* ought to be seen as a masked ball, in which 'figurative masks' become the most essential costumes. Shakespeare overstates and burlesques this theme in *Much Ado*, but is close to Castiglione in the general perception of courtly life as being similar to theatrical life.

The second common theme concerns the association of courtly behaviour with practical jokes. Bernardo Dovizi, usually referred to as Bibbiena, is given the task of outlining acceptable modes and idioms of courtly humour. He suggests that there are three main categories:

Now, to go back to the kind of pleasantries that pertain to our subject, I maintain that, in my opinion, there are three varieties, although Federico mentioned only two: namely, a long amusing narrative, in a polished style, that tells us how some incident was resolved; and the spontaneous thrust of a single cutting remark. But we shall add the third kind, called practical jokes, which include story-telling, brief comments, and also a certain amount of action.

The comedy in *Much Ado* comes more from spontaneous thrusts, for instance Beatrice and Benedick's dialogues, and practical jokes such as the gulling of Beatrice and Benedick, than from polished narratives. The hunting imagery Bernardo uses to define the practical joke is close to that used during the garden scenes in *Much Ado*, or indeed to that used during the practical joke played upon Malvolio in *Twelfth Night*:

a practical joke consists simply in an amicable deception regarding things that give little or no offence ... The first kind is when someone or other is cleverly tricked, in an adroit and amusing fashion; and the other is when, as it were, a net is spread and a little bait is offered, so that the victim causes his own downfall.

Benedick is a 'fowl' (II. iii. 94) who is being stalked by Don Pedro and the others. Beatrice is a fish who is being angled for by Hero and Ursula with 'false sweet bait' (III. i. 33). The examples that Bernardo goes on to cite do not have much bearing on *Much Ado*, except that in general terms they revolve around disguise. Castiglione is not the only writer who draws attention to the courtier as practical joker. Indeed, the discussion in *The Courtier* is rather sidetracked into a consideration of the morality of a particular joke that is played in Giovanni Boccaccio's *Decameron* (1353). It would be a mistake, then, to superimpose either dreary or cosy images of Court life on to the Renaissance Court. The Elizabethan Court, like other Renaissance ones, became more and more the centre for administration and the distribution of patronage. It was also the main location for spectacle, festivity and entertainment. The 'comic climate' of *Much Ado* is nevertheless signalled by the fact that practical jokes, pleasant and unpleasant, are not just *an* activity of courtly life but are rather *the* main activity.

Some popular stereotypes

Castiglione's *The Courtier* is a version of how Italians liked to represent themselves. The comic or villainous Italians who strutted across the Elizabethan and Jacobean stages probably owed more to popular pamphlets than they did to such refined courtesy literature. Thomas Nashe's *The Unfortunate Traveller* (1594) bristles with the same kind of popular prejudices against the Italianate as many of the plays. A banished English earl confesses:

Italy, the paradise of the earth and the epicure's heaven, how doth it form our young master? It makes him to kiss his hand like an ape, cringe his neck like a starveling, and play at Heypass, repass come aloft, when he salutes a man. From thence he brings the art of atheism, the art of epicurising, the art of whoring, the art of poisoning, the art of sodomitry. The only probable good thing they have to keep us from utterly condemning it is that it maketh a man an excellent courtier, a curious carpet knight; which is, by interpretation, a fine close lecher, a glorious hypocrite. It is now a privy note amongst the better sort of men, when they would set a singular mark or brand on a notorious villain, to say he hath been in Italy.

Nashe himself was probably never 'in Italy' but is not inhibited by such trifling considerations. This version of the Italianate, hand-kissing English courtier of dubious sexuality is similar to Michael Cassio. He too is a 'prattler' rather than a practitioner of anything else but vice. The Italians are also represented as being epicures, which carries associations of self-indulgence and gluttony. There are enough textual references to Benedick's 'epicurising' to suggest that he might have been played as a comic version of the Italian epicure during the first performances of *Much Ado*. Italy is seen as a land of drugs, but the familiar attack on Catholic damnation is transmuted into a more general one on atheism. There might even be hints of special pleading for Catholicism in Nashe's account of Italy, juxtaposed as it is with earlier descriptions of the follies of Puritan extremism. The narrator, flouting Jack Wilton, nevertheless has at least one unpleasant brush with Papal authority when the Pope's physician, Dr Zacharie, wants to use him as a human guinea pig. In general, Jack and his master, the Earl of Surrey, have the kind of thrills and spills that an English reader would have regarded as typical for an Italian journey: being imprisoned, escaping execution, being tricked or counterfeited and, of course, falling in love.

Hand-kissing and other courtly gestures clearly marked out the Italian courtier in the popular imagination, as well as the English one who tried to ape such an ape. Flamboyant, or what are referred to in *Much Ado* as 'exquisite' (I. iii. 46), clothes provided equally obvious signs of Italianate influences. The fashion for Italian fashions was created by the Earl of Oxford and other noblemen who went native on their travels. He became particularly attached to scented gloves. So apparently is Claudio, who sends Hero a pair of perfumed gloves to wear on her wedding day. The Royal Proclamations on Apparel suggest that the Italian craze was not just confined to noblemen like Oxford, but extended to all those with courtly ambitions and aspirations. Robert Greene's *A Quip for an Upstart Courtier* (1592) satirizes this trend. The narrator has a dream in which he sees a pair of Italian trousers striding down a hill:

The Netherstock was of the purest Granado silk: no cost was spared to set out these costly breeches, who had girt unto them a Rapier and Dagger gilt, point pendante, as quaintly as if some curious Florentine had tricked them up to square it up and down the streets before his Mistress. As these breeches were exceeding sumptuous to the eye, so were they passing pompous in their gestures, for they strutted up and down the Valley as proudly as though they had there appointed to act some desperate combat.

The clothes have literally become the man, or 'carpet knight'. These 'passing pompous' trousers have a date with 'a plain pair of Cloth-breeches' to dispute which of them has the right to clothe English manhood. The velvet and satin Italian trousers, who is 'whipt with gold twist' and 'interseamed with knots of pearl', has no doubts on this. His pedigree alone ought to settle the matter as he is

sprung from the ancient *Romans*, borne in *Italy*, the mistress of the world for chivalry, called into *England* from my native home (where I was famous) to honour your country and young Gentlemen here in *England* with my countenance ...

Cloth-breeches, who represents a truer form of gentility, regards him as an upstart and imposter:

And whereas thou sayest thou wert borne in *Italy*, & called hither by our courtiers, him may we curse that brought thee first into *England*: for thou camest not alone, but accompanied with multitude of abominable vices, hanging on thy bumbast nothing but infectious abuses, and vain glory, self love, sodomy and strange poisonings, wherewith thou has infected this glorious Island ...

The catalogue of Italian vices is a familiar one. The rest of the satire concerns the attempts to swear in a jury to try the case between the two pairs of trousers. It is directed more at abuses within the various professions and trades. The verdict is, needless to say, in favour of the homely and the homespun.

Much Ado moves through a number of potentially high, ceremonial moments: the welcome, the masked ball, the betrothal, the wedding, Claudio's repentance and the final dance. The critical and theatrical tendency has been to accept that, within the overall comic context, these scenes ought to be played with a certain dignity. Thus the suggestion is that only those parts of the play which involve Dogberry and the Watch can justifiably be classed as mock-ceremonial. According to this interpretation, *Much Ado* is close to the spirit of grand opera with elements of comic opera to provide light relief. Yet, if the play is set within its true Italianate context, it becomes easier to claim that comic opera and mock ceremonial dominate. There are some interesting parallels between the play and *The Courtier*, but the tone as a whole may be closer to that of the popular prejudice found in writers like Nashe and Greene.

Shakespeare had no qualms about scoring easy but effective dramatic points out of representing foreigners as being funny simply because they were foreigners. *Henry V* caricatures French accents as well as actions. This kind of basic comedy can be intensified on stage through extravagant gestures, such as hand-kissing, and flamboyant costumes. These ingredients come together in the splendidly ridiculous form of Monsieur Parolles in *All's Well That Ends Well*. It is thus entirely appropriate that this particular version of the 'curious carpet knight' should be upstaged by even funnier voices. The French Lords, doing all the voices, gull Parolles by pretending to be Russian, or at least alien, soldiers. Russian accents are also parodied in *Love's Labour's Lost* during the Masque of the Muscovites. In this kind of incident either the stage directions, explicit or implicit, or the text itself quite obviously calls for funny voices. Shakespeare's plays occasionally contain a whole part written out in a funny voice, for instance that of the French Doctor, Caius, in *The Merry Wives of Windsor*. The parts in *Much Ado* are not written down like this, but that does not necessarily mean that they were not played like this. It is even possible that snatches of Italian dialogue might have been ad-libbed into a particular part for comic effect. The text of *The Taming of the Shrew* retains just such a piece of Italian dialogue, which was probably lifted straight from Florio. Names can often supply an implicit set of stage directions as to how a particular part ought to be played. Nashe comes up with the best Italianate name: his Petro de Campo Frego takes a lot of beating. Yet, for an Elizabethan audience, Don Pedro of Arragon might have been in the same camp. Pedro, like Don Diego, was a familiar slang term of abuse for Spaniards in general, and for Arragon read arrogant. It is therefore possible for Don Pedro to contribute to the mock-ceremonial qualities of the play.

Machiavelli

Nashe satirizes Italian manners and morals in general, but his use of terms such as 'policy', 'stratagem' and 'counterfeit' takes the argument into a more specifically political dimension. For these were all terms that were particularly associated with Niccola Machiavelli's *The Prince*, which was probably completed towards the end of 1513. The English face of Machiavelli was a particularly sinister one and did much to reinforce prejudices against Italian ways of life and death. Machiavellian villains stalked the English stage in plays by Christopher Marlowe, Thomas Kyd,

Shakespeare and others, spying out 'advantage' and using a deadly mixture of 'cunning' and 'pretext' to gain it. The fact that few people had actually read *The Prince* was a trivial consideration. If Machiavelli the man did not exist, then Machiavelli the villain could be invented the more easily to satisfy the need for a name on which to hang all these anti-Italian prejudices. *The Prince*, especially in its early chapters, is a surprisingly conventional political manual when it is read rather than read about. Machiavelli, a career diplomat who was steeped in Classical history and philosophy, began in orthodox vein. He overstates some points which his contemporaries sometimes preferred to leave understated, for instance the need for effective military force to preserve the *status quo*:

The main foundations of every state . . . are good laws and good arms; and because you cannot have good laws without good arms, and where there are good arms, good laws inevitably follow, I shall not discuss laws but give my attention to arms.

Machiavelli was particularly wary of mercenary troops. Yet such a change of emphasis was hardly villainous or potentially revolutionary. Machiavelli the stage villain begins to reveal himself, however, towards the middle of the tract. He asserts, in what became an especially notorious chapter on 'How princes should honour their word', that truth has to be related to necessity:

a prudent ruler cannot, and should not, honour his word when it places him at a disadvantage and when the reasons for which he made his promise no longer exist. If all men were good, this precept would not be good; but because men are wretched creatures who would not keep their word to you, you need not keep your word to them.

Machiavelli has moved beyond the proposition that people let themselves be deceived to one which asserts that you have to deceive them before they deceive you. A prince is therefore under no compulsion to keep his word, although sometimes it may be to his 'advantage' to 'appear' to do so. This becomes part of a wider argument. Real generosity does not pay and real virtue can be ruinous, Machiavelli suggests, but the mere appearance of generosity and virtue costs nothing and may well purchase everything:

A prince, therefore, need not necessarily have all the good qualities I mentioned above, but he should certainly appear to have them. I would even go so far as to say that if he has these qualities and always behaves accordingly he will find them ruinous; if he only appears to have them they will render him service. He should appear to be compassionate, faithful to his word, guileless, and devout. And indeed he should be so. But his disposition should be such that, if he needs to be the opposite, he knows how.

Even such bold statements about political expediency do not, however, indicate why Machiavelli became the man they all loved to hate. He was criticized as much for what he did not say as for what he did say. The assumption behind such statements was that expediency was the ultimate court of appeal. Without ever stating it explicitly, he was rejecting Christian codes of morality and ethics. The fact that he did not even bother to mention them added considerable insult to the injury. Italians could be caricatured as Papists, but Machiavelli laid them open to the broader charge of atheism.

Machiavelli's concern with the manipulation of appearances means that he sees politics as a theatrical process:

Men in general judge by their eyes rather than by the hands; because everyone is in a position to watch few are in a position to come in close touch with you. Everyone sees what you appear to be, few experience what you really are ... The common people are always impressed by appearances and results.

He is dealing here with the theatrical relationship between the Court, or actors, and the country, or audience. His slogan 'everyone sees what you appear to be, few experience what you really are' nevertheless provides a very neat summary of the main themes of *Much Ado*. Comparisons between Shakespeare and Machiavelli are still too general on this point to be taken further. Perhaps Machiavelli's sinister reputation, together with some of the dubious associations conjured up by Italian locations, provided a general context for Shakespeare's very different treatment of this theme. More specifically, Shakespeare parodies the theatrical cult of the Machiavellian villain through Don John. This remarkably unsubtle villain has to be initiated into Italian finesse and cunning by Borachio.

Shakespeare and Spain

If Castiglione represented the velvet glove of the Italian Renaissance for the Elizabethans, Machiavelli became its iron fist. This 'might is right' interpretation ignored the patriotic call at the end of *The Prince* in which Lorenzo the Magnificent and others are urged to liberate Italy from the invaders and barbarians. Machiavelli could deal with ends as well as means, although one of the ends he had in mind was to find favour with the new Medicean government of Florence. Chief amongst these barbarians were the Spaniards. *Much Ado*'s debt to Italian sources, influences and images has been recognized if not always correctly interpreted. Its more specifically Spanish and Sicilian connections have not been explored. This is understandable since it seems likely that

Shakespeare inherited the Sicilian setting from Bandello. As indicated, the evidence suggests that Shakespeare's Sicily is less easily identifiable, historically and culturally, than Bandello's Sicily. Yet the fact that England was at war with Spain, which continued to rule Sicily, between 1585 and 1604, may in the end be more significant. The Elizabethans were closer to Machiavelli than they realized since Spain represented a common enemy. The 'Armada spirit' has been recognized as an important influence on the drama of the late 1580s and early 1590s. This may well have represented a high patriotic point, but the war and the propaganda that went with it dragged on. Sir Richard Grenville's death at 'Flores in the Azores' in 1591, immortalized in Tennyson's poem, was only one of a number of painful reminders that the defeat of the Armada in 1588 had not led to total victory. There were invasion scares throughout the 1590s and fears became heightened, albeit briefly, when Don John of Aquila landed in Ireland in 1601 with the intention of supporting Tyrone's uprising. Important Spanish exiles such as Antonio Perez became useful weapons in the propaganda offensive and the theatres continued to play a part in maintaining and sustaining anti-Spanish feeling. There was, for instance, a dramatization in 1599 of the Battle of Turnhout (1597) in which the Spanish forces in the Netherlands had been defeated.

It seems unlikely, therefore, that Spaniards were given an enthusiastic reception on the English stage during the whole of the 1590s. The braggart, boastful buffoon and comic dandy was a recognizable stage-type long before these Anglo-Spanish hostilities. Some of the bombastic captains who strutted across Elizabethan and Jacobean stages were not Spanish ones. Yet, in the cases where the braggart was closer to the stock part and therefore Spanish, he fulfilled the important need to ridicule the enemy. The misfortunes of Lazarillo de Tormes in Thomas Middleton's *Blurt, Master-Constable*, printed in 1602, fitted this particular bill. Don Adriano de Armado in *Love's Labour's Lost* is described by Navarre as

> *... a refined traveller of Spain;*
> *A man in all the world's new fashion planted,*
> *That hath a mint of phrases in his brain;*
> *One who the music of his own vain tongue*
> *Doth ravish like enchanting harmony;*
> *A man of compliments, whom right and wrong*
> *Have chose as umpire of their mutiny.*
>
> (I. i. 161–7)

Armado's attempts to dress fashionably, which include wearing a plumed feather in his hat, are paralleled by his desire to dress up his rhetoric. He is a walking dictionary who never uses one word when five are available. His attempts to 'mint' his own refined vocabulary comically rebound on him:

Sir, it is the King's most sweet pleasure and affection to congratulate the Princess at her pavilion in the posteriors of this day, which the rude multitude call the afternoon.

(V. i. 82–5)

Here and elsewhere Armado contrives to be ruder than the multitude. His costumes are scented and his gestures include hand-kissing and a strutting walk. He is a general version of the comic courtier, but his more specifically Spanish qualities centre around his boastfulness. He appears to be 'Most military sir' (V. i. 35). He is very attached to his rapier, which incidentally bears no relation to his wit, and swaggers around with his hand on its hilt. It is thus only natural that he should play the part of Hector in the Masque of the Nine Worthies. Yet, whilst he is playing this other great warrior, he is challenged to a duel by the swain Costard. True to the form of the Spanish braggart, he backs off and makes his excuses, which include the fact that he has no shirt on under his courtly finery. The braggart and dandy is comically exposed.

Armado's rhetorical attempts to be 'singled from the barbarous' indicate prejudices about Spanish obsessions with order and hierarchy. These obsessions are even more pronounced in the Prince of Arragon in *The Merchant of Venice*. He is the second suitor who tries to guess the riddle and win Portia. He rejects the gold casket because he does not want to be sullied by common desires:

> *I will not choose what many men desire,*
> *Because I will not jump with common spirits*
> *And rank me with the barbarous multitudes.*
> (II. ix. 31–3)

His speech as a whole is concerned with correct distinctions between 'the true seed of honour' and the 'low peasantry'. That other Prince of Arragon, Don Pedro, has many of the general attributes of the comic Italianate courtier. He may also have more specific affinities with an up-market version of the Spanish braggart. His reaction to Hero's supposed infidelity is so extreme because he sees it as a threat to his much-cherished honour. His silence during the middle parts of the denunciation scene, commented on specifically by Leonato, suggest a haughty aloofness:

LEONATO	*Sweet Prince, why speak not you?*
DON PEDRO	*What should I speak?*
	I stand dishonoured, that have gone about
	To link my dear friend to a common stale.

(IV. i. 61–3)

Hero has been transformed in his eyes from the Governor's daughter into a member of the 'rude' or 'barbarous' multitude. There are a number of ways of playing Antonio's comic challenge to Claudio. One of them is to cast both Claudio and Don Pedro as braggarts who back off, not out of reverence for Antonio, but because they are a little afraid of him. Antonio's challenge is, incidentally, triggered off because he thinks that Claudio is reaching for his rapier. It may be that Don Pedro and his gallants strut around the stage like Armado with their hands on their rapiers. Beatrice suggests that these gallants, particularly Benedick, are all mere prattlers when it comes to fighting. This is one of the instances when there is probably a great deal of 'matter' in her 'mirth'.

A pamphlet published in 1599, entitled *A Pageant of Spanish Humours*, which was translated from the Dutch, provides at least a clue as to how Spanish parts might be represented on stage, particularly in terms of presence and walk. The Spanish warrior is taken to task for being a braggart who is more concerned with show than substance:

Signior being in the street, or any other public place, his first gestures are to bend the head, turn the eye, and peacock-like to behold himself if nothing be amiss, his gait is like one who treads the measures, he scarce takes three steps, but the fourth, he again comtemplateth ... sometimes he will cast a leering eye aside, to spy if the beholders admire him not ... then he rouseth himself and expecteth a reverence of every one that passeth, he twisteth his moustachioes and strokes his beard.

The text of *Much Ado* indicates that both Don Pedro and Claudio dress like peacocks. Perhaps it is therefore not being too fanciful to suggest that at times they ought to walk like them as well.

Although the defeat of the Spanish Armada by what Richard Hakluyt described as 'nimble steerage' did not end hostilities, it nevertheless provided plenty of evidence to reinforce the stereotype of the Spanish braggart. Some pamphlets, for instance *A Fig for the Spaniard or Spanish Spirits* (1591), concentrated on the discrepancy between Spanish confidence on the European political and military stage and the chaos backstage. Variations on the phrase 'fig for the Spaniard' were, incidentally, quite common stage oaths, which were usually accompanied by gestures of the 'up yours' type. Pistol in Shakespeare's English history plays and Bosala in *The Duchess of Malfi* both use them. Other pamphlets merely combed descriptions of the Armada itself for examples of boastful or vainglorious warriors. Robert Greene's *The Spanish Masquerado* (1589) stirs most of the anti-Spanish prejudices into the pot. Philip II has been trapped since infancy 'in the darke and obscure dungeon of Papistry' and thus is ruled by his clergy. They in turn are seen as prisoners of their sodomy, lechery and gluttony. Greene then draws attention to the boastful nature of Spanish soldiers, in particular to that of Don Pedro de Valdes:

he was one of the first that was taken, not making any resistance at all, or shewing any point of honourable resolution, not so much as drawing his sword in defence. Is this the mind of a Nobleman of dubbed Chivalry? Of a Captain, to submit in the first extremity? Do the Spaniards prize life so high, that they make no estimation of honour? ... He that like a Lion came storming from Spain, humbly like a lamb crouched to our Admiral in the English seas, yielding himself and his prisoners: Now note the Spanish braving promises, what cowardly conclusions they infer.

The Messenger in *Much Ado* describes Claudio as 'doing, in the figure of a lamb, the feats of a lion' (I. i. 14–15), Greene claims that Don Pedro de Valdes did the exact opposite. There are conflicting historical accounts of Don Pedro's performance, or lack of it, during the early stages of the Armada confrontation, although Greene's caricature version seems to be quite close to the mark. Don Pedro voted for a quick attack, whereas the majority of the other leaders favoured caution. He was also renowned for his quarrelsome nature. Relations in the Armada were soured by the vendetta between Don Pedro and his cousin, Don Diego de Valdes. Don Pedro's flagship was involved in a collision with two other Spanish ships before battle had been engaged with the English fleet. He was therefore forced to retire from the battle formation. The accounts become a bit hazy here, but it seems that the Spanish command, perhaps influenced by Don Diego, decided to leave him where he was rather than send help. He interpreted this as an insult to his honour and refused to take any further part in the campaign. He was still standing on his dignity when Sir Francis Drake captured the flagship the next morning. He made a chivalrous speech of surrender and was taken prisoner. He remained in captivity in England until 1593, when he was released in the vain hope that he might be part of a diplomatic initiative to solve Anglo-Spanish problems. This arrogant Don Pedro was given an audience by Queen Elizabeth as well as a dinner by the Lord Mayor of London before he went home to continue his family feud.

Messina provided both ships and supplies for the Armada, although some of them were destroyed by Drake at Cadiz before the Spaniards set sail. The Sicilians, then as now, had a general reputation for volcanic temperament and forms of brigandage. They were also seen, even by their Spanish rulers, as taking ceremony so seriously as to reduce it to absurdity. In the words of a modern historian,

Sicilians became celebrated for their hand kissing, cap doffing and gaming. Their preoccupation with precedence, decorum and ceremonial went on being ascribed by themselves to the example of Spain, but in practice a code of gallantry, gravity and etiquette was taken to such an extreme as to appear odd even to the Spanish.

This obsession with ceremony was probably the result of Sicily's decline during the sixteenth century. Its reputation as the 'granary' of the Spanish Empire did not necessarily bring economic benefits to the island itself and, intellectually, it was rightly regarded as something of a backwater. Its glories were all in the past, particularly the Anglo-Norman past. Ceremony is usually the last refuge of the declining power. The Sicilians did not so much stand on it as clutch at it. Thus modern productions of *Much Ado* which play the ceremonial parts reverently in the belief that this is historically authentic may be wide of the mark. The contextual evidence is admittedly rather sketchy, but there is enough textual evidence to suggest that Leonato may reduce ceremony to absurdity through overplaying it.

Messina may have carried an even more specific set of associations for Shakespeare's audiences. It was the port from which the fleet of the Holy League set sail in 1571 to fight the great sea battle of Lepanto with the Turks. This fleet was commanded by Don John of Austria. The citizens of Messina paid their own tribute to this conquering hero by building the famous Strada d'Austria in his honour. As suggested, a study of the sources for *Much Ado* indicates that Don John is an addition to the basic story-line. His name, together with the Messinese connections, may be a completely coincidental and therefore an innocent choice. It is still worth considering the alternative explanation, even though it is based more on the play's own logic than on that of history.

Don John of Austria was one of the most charismatic figures of the counter-reformation. He was, or rather was supposed to be, a bastard son of Charles V. Charles's successor Philip II, came to rely heavily on his brother's abilities as an imperial trouble-shooter. Whereas Philip was distant, devout and diligent, Don John was open, extrovert and hungry for personal military glory. He achieved this, together with a reputation for severity, when he was put in charge of crushing the Moorish, or Morisco, uprising in Spain. He was then appointed Captain-General of the Sea and given command of the Holy League fleet. When he arrived in Messina at the end of August 1571, he found the fleet suffering from the kinds of divisions and uncertainties which surrounded the Holy League itself. He nevertheless quickly managed to weld it together into an almost unique fighting force. His instructions were to contain the Turks, which did not rule out an essentially defensive campaign. He felt that attack was the best form of defence and sailed out of Messina in September to sweep the sea for his enemy. The two fleets eventually found each other and engaged in battle on 7 October 1571. Although Don John inflicted a crushing defeat on the Turks, historians have always been unsure about both the short- and long-term effects of Lepanto. It certainly did not halt Turkish advances in the Mediterranean, particularly along the African coast. Perhaps it needs to be seen as a great psychological and symbolic victory, which Philip and others failed to capitalize upon because of more pressing problems.

Apart from sharing the same name and both being bastards, Shakespeare's Don John and the historical Don John have precious little in common. This could, however, be the point if the inverted logic of parody is followed. Shakespeare's Don John loses battles, whereas his more illustrious namesake was renowned for winning them. Shakespeare's Don John is withdrawn and melancholic, whereas the historical one was charming and dynamic. These and other polarities suggest a process of comic inversion. Heroic qualities in general are being mocked. More specifically, the Spaniards are being mocked because Don John, whose reputation continued long after his death in 1578, was one of the most charismatic leaders that they had ever had at their disposal.

Even if this particular piece of the contextual jigsaw is rejected for being too speculative, the picture which emerges suggests that *Much Ado* is a mock-ceremonial play which also chauvinistically deflates the heroic pretensions as well as the manners and mannerisms of both Italians and Spaniards. Its climate is nevertheless a comic rather than a darkly satirical one. There are some similarities between Shakespeare's representation of Spaniards in *Much Ado* and Jonson's in *The Alchemist*, which was first performed in 1610. Yet there are fundamental differences between Shakespeare's brand of festive comedy and Jonson's satirical morality plays, just as there are some important differences between Shakespeare's and Webster's representations of Italy. The context suggests mockery and deflation, but only the text itself can establish their function and tone.

Part Three: Texts

5 Don John and Dogberry

Transgression and redemption

Don John plays the transgressor, whilst Dogberry plays the redeemer. Play is, once again, the operative word. For instance, Dogberry himself does nothing in this role even though he makes much ado about it. He is not present at the arrest and it is Verges who first breaks the news of it to Leonato. The Sexton saves the trial from complete farce and it is Borachio rather than Dogberry who tells everybody of its result. Similarly, Don John is not particularly effective in his role. The play opens with the news of his failure to undermine his brother's authority. His first plot against Claudio backfires. He has another go at playing the villain, but needs a lot of stage coaching from Borachio. He runs away when things start to go wrong and is not even very good at this as he gets caught almost immediately. Potentially serious themes of transgression and redemption are burlesqued by making these two incompetents the vehicles for them. Neither of them is present at the end of the play: Don John is in his brother's custody and Dogberry has presumably gone home to admire his gowns and to read the statutes. Their absence confirms the comic nature of the treatment of these themes.

Don John and Dogberry appear at first sight to be worlds apart. Don John likes to cause trouble. whereas Dogberry and the Watch go out of their way to avoid giving offence. Don John is a grandee, whereas Dogberry comes from, or likes to believe that he comes from, a professional middle class. Some of the comedy is generated by the fact that foreigners are upstaged by English eccentricity. Such differences are, however, rather deceptive. Both of them mock ceremony: Don John by trying to disrupt it and Dogberry by trying to imitate it. Also, Dogberry may be from outside courtly circles, but he positively revels in his contacts with them. Don John is obsessed by order and protocol. He dislikes Claudio, and probably Hero as well, because he sees them as social climbers. Dogberry, both in his briefing to the Watch and in his conduct of the trial, shows a similar concern for order and protocol. The transgressor and the redeemer also both carry their self-importance within this order to excessive, comic extremes.

Don John as comic villain

If Don John is conspicuous by his absence from the last scene, he is almost conspicuous by his presence at the beginning of the play. He should be dressed in black and thus in stark contrast to the dedicated followers of fashion. He also stands out from the fashionable crowd by refusing to engage in the wordplay which passes for wit in Messina. Leonato enjoys playing the role of host and, perhaps, takes the etiquette of it to Sicilian extremes. He extends his flamboyant welcome to victor and vanquished alike:

LEONATO *Let me bid you welcome, my Lord, being reconciled to the Prince your brother. I owe you all duty.*
DON JOHN *I thank you. I am not of many words, but I thank you.*

(I. i. 145–9)

Here and later on Don John's public part, or mask, is that of the plain speaker, which usually carries associations of plain dealing as well. His attempt to continue playing this part after his unsuccessful rebellion, together with the fact that he nearly gets away with it, has a certain amount of comic potential. Like Iago, he trades on a reputation for bluff, manly honesty. Unlike Iago, this cover is blown, or ought to be, from the word go. Don John carries on playing his part, but even in doing so almost gives the game away. Three of his few words are 'I' which, far from offering a convincing performance as plain dealer, suggest his continuing self-obsession.

This give-away hint becomes blatantly obvious when Don John exits from the public stage for a behind-the-scenes conference with his companions, Conrade and Borachio:

I cannot hide what I am. I must be sad when I have cause, and smile at no man's jests; eat when I have stomach, and wait for no man's leisure; sleep when I am drowsy, and tend on no man's business; laugh when I am merry, and claw no man in his humour.

(I. iii. 12–17)

Interpretations of *Much Ado* which suggest that Don John casts a dark, problematic shadow over the proceedings ignore the extent to which he himself is a comic character. The comedy works on at least three levels in this scene. First of all, somebody who has introduced himself as a man of few words is unable to stop talking about himself. Secondly, his statement 'I cannot hide what I am' is rich in irony. He is not a convincing actor in the part of plain speaker, but at least he is trying to hide what he is. Thirdly, he needs help from Conrade and Borachio to make these public performances a little more convincing. Conrade has to give him a quick lesson in Machiavellian principles:

Yea, but you must not make the full show of this till you may do it without controlment. You have of late stood out against your brother, and he hath ta'en you newly into his grace, where it is impossible you should take true root but by the fair weather that you make yourself; it is needful that you frame the season for your own harvest.

(I. iii. 18–24)

The boss has to be bossed about. He is the stooge and Conrade and Borachio the masters. He needs these little touches of Italianate finesse and cunning to play his part successfully.

He is just a bit too slow on the uptake to be taken seriously as a serious villain. Borachio brings the news of the intended marriage between Claudio and Hero, but has to work quite hard to explain the plot against it to the boss:

BORACHIO   *I can, at any unseasonable instant of the night, appoint her to look out at her lady's chamber-window.*

DON JOHN   *What life is in that, to be the death of this marriage?*

BORACHIO   *The poison of that lies in you to temper. Go you to the Prince your brother; spare not to tell him that he hath wronged his honour in marrying the renowned Claudio – whose estimation do you mightily hold up – to a contaminated stale, such a one as Hero.*

DON JOHN   *What proof shall I make of that?*

BORACHIO   *Proof enough to misuse the Prince, to vex Claudio, to undo Hero and kill Leonato.*

(II. ii 15–26)

Borachio not only comes up with the plot, but also spells out Don John's part in it. He tells the boss not to give the game away by attacking Claudio. The lines should be that Claudio is 'renowned', and I have a great 'estimation' for him, which is why I am bringing you this sad news. Real villains, like Richard III and Iago, use and abuse their accomplices along with everybody else. *Much Ado* offers a comic inversion of this relationship: Roderigo becomes the brains behind Iago and Buckingham manipulates Richard. Dogberry and Don John are both so self-obsessed that they are ignorant of their own limitations, which include ignorance and stupidity.

Don John's motives are not such a serious issue if he is part of the play's comedy. He has a melancholic frame of mind which needs to feed off other people's misfortunes. His comic brand of malignity can therefore be seen as fundamentally motiveless. The fact that, like Iago, he offers several motives for his actions raises doubts about the authenticity of any of them. Don Pedro is a compulsive player of games, whereas he is a compulsive maker of mischief, a spoilt spoiler of the other child's fun. Part of his grievance against Claudio is that the younger man has become his brother's playmate. He also dislikes the whole idea of marriage, claiming that only fools will betroth themselves to such 'unquietness' (I. iii. 44). At one level, marriage symbolizes an adult world from which his childish antics necessarily exclude him. At a more serious level, the fact that he is illegitimate means that marriage symbolizes his exclusion from supposedly decent society. He provides a constant reminder that 'chaste constancy' in marriage is at best an ideal, at worst a deceitful mask. The theme is a serious one, but it is played for its comic variations in *Much Ado*. Don John the bastard is too obsessed by order and degree. Part of his grievance against Claudio is that the young man is a 'start-up' (I. iii. 61). Claudio may be a count, but he is not in the same social league as a prince of the blood. The comedy, cruel as it so often is, comes from the fact that the illegitimate Don John sets himself up as the arbiter of the legitimacy, or otherwise, of social relationships. He comes from the wrong side of the proverbial blanket, but is quick to spot anyone from the wrong side of the tracks. It is possible that this social snobbery extends to Hero as well as to Claudio:

BORACHIO *Marry, it is your brother's right hand.*
DON JOHN *Who? The most exquisite Claudio?*
BORACHIO *Even he.*
DON JOHN *A proper squire! And who, and who? Which way looks he?*
BORACHIO *Marry, on Hero, the daughter and heir of Leonato.*
DON JOHN *A very forward March-chick! How came you to this?*

(I. iii. 45–53)

Most editors suggest, probably correctly, that this 'very forward March-chick' is Claudio. It can, however, be taken as a reference to Hero, in which case she too is being accused of being socially pushy or 'forward'. Claudio may not be fit company for a prince, but even his worst enemy would agree that he was a cut above a mere governor's daughter. Don John implies that the wedding is much ado about nothing because, compared with his princely self, the participants are both nothings. This exchange between Borachio and Don John provides another example of his lack of Italianate subtlety. He is morosely passive until activated by his accomplices. Once again, things have to be spelt out for him. Don

John is on stage when Claudio eyes up Hero, who is anyway the obvious and perhaps only candidate, but fails to notice what takes place. Real villains like Richard III and Iago are able to orchestrate, improvise and anticipate. Ironically, Don John, who with Borachio goes on to deceive the 'very eyes' (V. i. 221) of Claudio and Don Pedro, is not very good at keeping his own open. Like Dogberry and the Watch, he does not watch what is happening.

The reference to Hero's lack of legitimate social credentials becomes much more explicit immediately after the masked ball. Don John, perhaps pointed in the right direction by Borachio, pretends to mistake Claudio for Benedick. He tells him that Don Pedro wants Hero:

Signor, you are very near my brother in his love. He is enamoured on Hero; I pray you dissuade him from her; she is no equal for his birth. You may do the part of an honest man in it.

(II. i. 148 51)

Under the circumstances, his advice to Claudio to play 'the part of an honest man' is rich in irony. It is not just that Don John is trying to be devious and dishonest. It is also that he almost signals that this is what he is doing by stating so explicitly that honesty is merely another part to be acted. His foot is uncomfortably close to his mouth. He has another stab at playing 'the part of an honest man' when he breaks the news of Hero's supposed infidelity to Claudio and Don Pedro. He remembers Borachio's advice to play up his 'estimation' for Claudio, but makes rather an awkward job of it:

CLAUDIO   *If there be any impediment, I pray you discover it.*
DON JOHN   *You may think I love you not; let that appear hereafter, and*
   aim better at me by that I now will manifest. For my brother,
   I think he holds you well, and in dearness of heart hath holp to
   effect your ensuing marriage – surely suit ill spent, and labour
   ill bestowed!

(III.ii. 83–9)

He knows that his brother has a high opinion of Claudio, so 'think' carries a hint of disapproval which is inappropriate for the occasion. It may be that in giving a 'circumstances shortened' (III. ii. 91–2) version of events he is making a virtue out of necessity. The part of man of few words, although entirely in keeping with the role of the plain dealer, may nevertheless be forced on him as he is not very good at remembering the lines that Borachio has written for him. That Don Pedro and Claudio fall for his clumsy presentation is a result of their failure rather than his success. Once again, the foot is in the mouth. Don John is supposed to be proving that he is a reformed character but his choice of words, for instance describing Hero as 'disloyal' (III. ii. 93), provides uncomfortable and probably unnecessary reminders of his past conduct. His bluff, double bluff is always in danger of being called, ironically by himself. It would be dangerous to spend too much time wondering why Don Pedro and Claudio are so gullible. The 'comic climate' of the play establishes a world of extreme or excessive gullibility. The answer to the question of why Hamlet does not behave like Fortinbras is that there would be no play if he did so. Similarly, Don Pedro and Claudio are denied access to the shortest route out of the maze. To treat the point more seriously, Don John is believed because he is a man. Masculine and feminine spheres are sharply divided. The men have spent too much time fighting with or against each other ever to be at ease in the feminine or domestic sphere. The jokes about marital infidelity are a way of articulating, but also trying to contain, this basic unease. The evidence against Don John is quite strong: his rebellion has just been put down and Claudio knows that he told a lie at the end of the masked ball. Yet he is believed because he is an old soldier, even though his mask of honesty is in danger of slipping right off. The levels of gullibility in *Othello* are more complex, although at its crudest General Othello trusts Ancient (or Ensign) Iago rather than his wife. Messinese society as a whole expects men to tell the truth, with the corollary that it is not surprised if women turn out to be liars. Leonato rejects Hero so quickly during the denunciation scene because he is unable to believe that his male guests, particularly such distinguished ones, could tell a lie:

> *Would the two Princes lie, and Claudio lie,*
> *Who loved her so, that, speaking of her foulness,*
> *Washed it with tears? Hence from her, let her die!*
> (IV. i. 150–52)

The separation between male and female is so great that Leonato questions the word of his daughter rather than that of Don John, even though this Prince ought to have forfeited any claims to be a reliable witness.

Don John's performance during the denunciation scene once again almost draws too much attention to itself as a performance. He moves in surprisingly quickly to stop anybody following up Don Pedro's remark that Hero's lover had confessed to a long-standing relationship. Yet his choice of words is unfortunate to put it mildly:

> *Fie, fie, they are not to be named, my lord,*

> *Not to be spoke of!*
> *There is not chastity enough in language*
> *Without offence to utter them. Thus, pretty lady,*
> *I am sorry for thy much misgovernment.*
>
> (IV. i. 93–7)

He produces the banana-skins and nearly falls flat on his face. The bastard starts defending chastity and the rebel accuses somebody else of 'misgovernment'. His other intervention is just as clumsy. Don Pedro is standing on his own dignity and Leonato is thrashing around trying to get some responses to clarify his own:

LEONATO *Are these things spoken, or do I but dream?*
DON JOHN *Sir, they are spoken, and these things are true.*

> (IV. i. 64–5)

The inexperienced slanderer chooses a very delicate moment in the proceedings to come out with the perfect definition of slander. The mask slips once more but nobody notices.

    Much Ado very self-consciously draws attention to its own theatricality. Don John tries to play the part of a subtle, Machiavellian villain but, even with more than a little help from his friends, turns in a comically coarse performance. He is meant to be a slippery-tongued schemer, but his slips of the tongue reveal that he is miscast. Dogberry is not the only comic character who has problems with words. Don John is, quite simply, a comic character because he is quite simple. The comedy he generates early on in the play is quite broad, although it is accompanied by more ironic touches. This bastard stands up for chastity.

Don John and Don Pedro

There are a number of obvious differences between the two brothers. Don Pedro is legitimate, whereas his brother is not. He wins the battles that Don John loses. Their stage presences also conflict. The sombrely dressed Don John is eclipsed by his brother's splendid apparel. Beatrice draws attention to Don Pedro's dandyism in her mocking refusal of his mock-proposal:

No, my lord, unless I might have another for working-days: your grace is too costly to wear every day.

> (II. i. 302–4)

The similarities between the two brothers are more significant than these differences. They both suffer from melancholia, although they employ different remedies. Don Pedro doses himself up with wordplay and practical jokes, whereas Don John takes his mischief-making pills. Both men require assistance from their young men. Don Pedro cracks jokes with Benedick and Claudio, whilst Don John plots with Borachio and Conrade. They are both unmarried, middle-aged men whose life is centred around themselves and those who might reflect their glory. They appear to disagree over marriage. Don John is against it, whilst Don Pedro devotes a lot of his hyperactive energy to trying to promote it. Like everything else, it is all a game to this playful Prince. Don John makes mischief out of it, whilst Don Pedro regards it as excellent sport. The pleasure comes partly from the fact that he is never going to play the game for real. Bachelors like Benedick may come and go, but he will go on for ever. There is a parallel with the activities of Antonio in *The Merchant of Venice*. He puts up the collateral so that his young friend, Bassanio, can go to Belmont and beat the Duke of Arragon and the others for Portia's hand. He loves Bassanio but reconciles himself to the idea of his friend's marriage. It has been suggested that his 'feminine' characteristics manifest themselves in his compulsive gambling, risking all the world to nothing on his argosies and ventures. His decision to equip Bassanio for his romantic voyage to Belmont can also be interpreted as a reckless gamble. The argument is fraught with problems of gender stereotyping. It implies, however, that gambling, whilst obviously not being an exclusively feminine activity, nevertheless provides Antonio with a dramatic but no less sublimated way of rejecting a masculine world of prudent marriage and investment. Don Pedro's practical jokes may fulfil a similar function. The decision to gull both Beatrice and Benedick is a reckless one, particularly as every wall and arrass in Messina seems to have ears. Don Pedro is promoting a marriage, but the way he goes about it suggests a certain antipathy to the institution. Similarly, he discharges his conventional responsibilities towards Claudio by discussing Hero's marriage with her father. Yet he nearly undermines this conventional role by insisting on playing a more unconventional one at the masked ball.

Don Pedro decides to pack his bags and leave when the marriage game starts to get serious. It produces melancholic as well as festive responses from him. His decision to look for new sport comes just before Don John's accusations:

DON PEDRO *I do but stay till your marriage be consummate, and then go*
I toward Arragon.

CLAUDIO *I'll bring you thither, my lord, if you'll vouchsafe me.*

DON PEDRO *Nay, that would be as great a soil in the new gloss of your*

*marriage as to show a child his new coat and forbid him to
wear it. I will only be bold with Benedick for his company;
for, from the crown of his head to the sole of his foot, he is all
mirth; he hath twice or thrice cut Cupid's bow-string and the
little hangman dare not shoot at him.*

(III. ii. 1–11)

As the distinctly mirthless, lovesick Benedick is on stage at the time, this
little play is probably acted out for his benefit. It may nevertheless still be
true that Don Pedro hopes that Benedick is not going to join Claudio as
a deserter from the ranks of male friendship. His imagery reveals a certain
distaste for marriage: it is like a child's new coat, fun to wear until the
novelty wears off or out. If Benedick is associated with, and associates
himself with, food imagery, Don Pedro is often decked out in clothes
imagery. Don John tries to wear the mask of an honest man, whilst his
brother dons one more appropriate to a festive master of revels. Don
Pedro is the more accomplished actor, a genuine comedy turn rather than
a part that merely generates comedy. He is a splendid mimic, giving
an impersonation of Beatrice for Benedick's benefit and sending up
Dogberry's attempts to cultivate legal and rhetorical jargon. Yet his mask
slips as well, both before and after the denunciation scene. He is booked
in for at least a month of fun and games at Leonato's house, but marriage
casts its shadow over his holiday plans. Perhaps he also just needs to keep
on the move, physically as well as verbally. The way to combat 'high-
proof melancholy' (V. i. 122) is to leave no time for introspection. Much
ado, or a series of festive games, provides some escape from gloomy
thoughts about nothingness.

Critics have been so concerned with the problems that Don John is
supposed to create for the play's comic tone, that they tend to overlook
the fact that Don Pedro is the more problematic character. He starts off
being the life and soul of the party, but by the end of the play his satires
and epigrams are a bit contaminated and stale. Benedick does not
return to Aragon and sends his former mentor back there with a few home
truths:

I'll tell thee what, Prince; a college of wit-crackers cannot flout me out of my
humour. Dost thou think I care for a satire or an epigram? No; if a man will be
beaten with brains, 'a shall wear nothing handsome about him.

(V. iv. 99 103)

Don John's court has already been split up. The boss is in custody and
his two accomplices are presumably in prison. Their fate is left unclear,
as indeed is the precise nature of the charge against them, which is in

keeping with the burlesque interpretation of transgression and redemption. Don Pedro's court is splitting up. Claudio and Benedick dance with their brides-to-be, but Don Pedro is unable to join this particular party. He led the revellers in the masked ball yet has to sit this one out. Benedick's festive commentary may not produce a particularly festive response:

Prince, thou art sad; get thee a wife, get thee a wife. There is no staff more reverend than one tipped with horn.

(V. iv. 120–22)

Benedick is very much the life and soul of this party, stealing the show from Don Pedro. When the news of Don John's arrest is brought, he takes it upon himself to advise Don Pedro on the appropriate 'punishments' (V. iv. 126) after the wedding. His advice to Don Pedro to get himself a wife is itself quite a punishing and potentially cruel remark. It should be fairly obvious to everyone that this camp, middle-aged bachelor will return to Aragon to find another clutch of impressionable, younger men. Don John increases and intensifies the play's comedy. So does his brother, perhaps until he becomes the butt of the joke.

Elizabethan clowning

Elizabethan comedy has become words on a page. Readings that are aware of production and performance can try to put these words back on the stage. There is still a danger, however, of the comedy being defined in verbal rather than visual terms. Much has been written about Elizabethan wordplay, not enough about theatrical horseplay. Expression, gesture, costume and movement can all be used to support the verbal comedy, or else as comic devices in their own right. Kempe inherited the mantle of King of Comedy from Dick Tarlton, who acted for the Queen's Men in the 1580s. The evidence indicates that Tarlton could raise a laugh simply by slowly raising the trap door in the middle of the stage and staring at the audience with a deadpan expression. He made them laugh by refusing to do so himself. The clown's entrance might involve other visual tricks. Their costume often consisted of baggy trousers, known as giant's hose, and enormous shoes or boots. Elizabethan comedy involved clowns tripping up and falling over, as well as verbal trips and stumbles. The only textual clue as to what Kempe might have worn when playing the part of Dogberry is the stage direction to IV. II: 'Enter Dogberry, Verges and the Sexton in gowns'. Modern productions tend to put Dogberry into sober, nondescript fustian clothes. It may be that, on the Elizabethan stage, the comedy was much broader with Dogberry wearing the traditional costume of the clown underneath his much-cherished gown. The outward appearance of the gown only just disguises, or masks, the person of the clown.

Fashion and fashioning, or dressing up events, are major themes in *Much Ado*. One of the longest variations on the 'fashion is the fashion' (III. iii. 119) theme takes place when the drunken Borachio confesses to Conrade, and to the Watch, his part in Don John's production. The performance itself obviously provides an illustration of the theme: Margaret becomes Hero because she is dressed like her. Borachio is reluctant at first to talk about the play. Indeed he has, figuratively speaking, already changed costumes. He is no longer the Machiavellian villain but plays the honest man. There is plenty of comic potential, rarely exploited, in the speed of his conversion. At a more serious level, it provides another example of the play's heightened theatricality by allowing parts and roles to be more important than the development and consistency of a 'character'. Iago refuses to answer his accusers at the end of *Othello*, whereas Borachio during and after the trial scene tells them everything. His confession to Conrade takes the form of clichéd statements about fashion stealing and thus becoming personality, which only refer indirectly to what has just taken place:

Seest thou not, I say, what a deformed thief this fashion is, how giddily 'a turns about all the hot bloods between fourteen and five-and-thirty, sometimes fashioning them like Pharaoh's soldiers in the reechy painting, sometime like god Bel's priests in the old church-window, sometime like the shaven Hercules in the smirched worm-eaten tapestry, where his codpiece seems as massy as his club?

(III. iii. 127–34)

Part of the comedy springs from the fact that, in dramatic context, these observations are themselves fashionable disguises which, at best, only hint at the truth. As Conrade puts it:

All this I see; and I see that the fashion wears out more apparel than the man. But art not thou thyself giddy with the fashion too, that thou hast shifted out of thy tale into telling me of the fashion?

(III. iii. 135–8)

The comedy is intensified by the fact that Borachio's costume change has been figurative rather than literal. If both he and the gentlemanly Conrade are visualized as being dressed in Italianate fashions, then the permutations on the fashion theme become greater. Two Italian dandies are ironically discussing the shortcomings of fashion. One of these dandies, Borachio, is dressed in a costume appropriate for the part of a sensual, selfish Latin lover, even though he is now playing the part of a sentimental, altruistic lover of justice. The reformed thief is not instantly recognizable thanks to a 'deformed thief' called fashion.

Conrade accuses Borachio of padding out his confession. It is also padding in a more specifically theatrical sense since it gives the Watch a chance to go through their comic paces. They make some verbal asides whilst they eavesdrop on this conversation between Borachio and Conrade, but their comedy has to be visual rather than verbal. It is difficult to recover a sense of how Elizabethan comics might have filled out, perhaps even padded out, this particular gap in the written text. Their stage props would have included 'bills', or pike-shaped staffs, and lanterns. These could be dropped or tripped over, all but alerting Borachio to the fact that he is still putting on a performance for an audience. A more interesting way of playing it might be to let the Watch play the part of the audience much more self-consciously. Elizabethan playwrights often criticized the 'groundlings' for cracking jokes or nuts and thus interrupting a performance. The Watch might 'stand close' (III. iii. 105) to the two performers themselves acting the part of rather a slow audience. If they do pay attention to the play, they still misunderstand it:

BORACHIO	*But seest thou not what a deformed thief this fashion is?*
FIRST WATCHMAN	(aside) *I know that Deformed; 'a has been a vile thief this seven year; 'a goes up and down like a gentleman. I remember his name.*
BORACHIO	*Didst thou not hear somebody?*
CONRADE	*No; 'twas the vane on the house.*

(III. iii. 120–26)

If the Watch are a self-conscious rather than a clumsily furtive audience, then they too can emphasize *Much Ado*'s theatricality.

Given Shakespeare's reputation for wordplay, comparisons between his comedies and silent cinema might seem to be singularly inappropriate ones. Yet Tarlton's Buster Keaton face, Kempe's Chaplinesque dress and, perhaps, the Watch's Keystone capers, all suggest that Shakespeare needs to be set within a visual as well as a verbal tradition of comedy. The text suggests that Verges is little, whereas Dogberry is large, a classic combination for the double act. Verges's name derives from his staff of office rather than from the French for orchard or indeed the English for a grass border. Comedy can therefore be generated by having this little old man almost literally bowed down under the weight of this staff. Dogberry's failure to help him out can be used as a visual reminder of the Master Constable's self-importance. Stage walks can also provide this kind of visual shorthand. Verges probably shuffles along in front with quick, little steps, whilst Dogberry's tread is more measured to suit his more important rank. Leonato's brother, Antonio, is the best candidate for that old theatrical favourite, the 'silly walk'. He is what the Elizabethans, drawing on *commedia dell'arte* traditions, called a pantaloon or comic old man. He thus has some similarities with Gremio in *The Taming of the Shrew*. His participation in the masked ball is a comic turn. He is instantly recognized by Ursula because of his 'waggling' head and 'dry hand' (II. i. 102 and 105). He may also have an idiosyncratic, or just old-fashioned, style of dancing. He is wheeled on, perhaps even literally, for another turn after the denunciation scene. He tells Leonato to keep calm, but then loses his own cool at the sight of Don Pedro and Claudio. His attempt to challenge Claudio to a duel should get close to slapstick comedy. It also provides an example of the way in which *Much Ado* burlesques the Italianate for the comic old man tries to become the hot-blooded avenger:

ANTONIO *Come, follow me, boy; come, sir boy, come, follow me;*
          Sir boy, I'll whip you from your foining fence;
          Nay, as I am a gentleman, I will.
LEONATO *Brother—*
ANTONIO *Content yourself. God knows I loved my niece;*
          And she is dead, slandered to death by villains,
          That dare as well answer a man indeed
          As I dare take a serpent by the tongue.
          Boys, apes, braggarts, Jacks, milksops!
LEONATO   *Brother Antony—*
ANTONIO *Hold you content. What, man! I know them, yea,*
          And what they weigh, even to the utmost scruple—
          Scrambling, out-facing, fashion-monging boys,
          That lie and cog and flout, deprave and slander,
          Go anticly, show outward hideousness,
          And speak off half a dozen dangerous words,
          How they might hurt their enemies, if they durst;
          And this is all.
LEONATO *But, brother Antony—*
ANTONIO   *Come, 'tis no matter;*
          Do not you meddle, let me deal in this.

                                     (V. i. 83–101)

Roles have become comically reversed. Leonato now attempts to restrain Antonio. As suggested earlier, heroic roles may be reversed as well with

Don Pedro and Claudio being just a little bit anxious in case Antonio really means what he says. The comedy, unlike Antonio's old sword, is double-edged. There are no explicit stage directions to accompany this comic challenge which is why critics whose approach is primarily verbal have missed its potential. It is not that difficult, however, to write in some of these directions: Antonio attempts to draw his sword but falls over in the process, or aims a thrust at Claudio but hits Leonato instead. The comedy swordfight was an established routine in which the participants would be expected to pad out the text with visual stage business. Shakespeare uses it, even more effectively, in *Twelfth Night* where the cowardly Sir Andrew Aguecheek and the totally inexperienced Viola reluctantly square up for a duel. The fight between the comic Frenchman Caius and the comic Welshman Evans in *The Merry Wives of Windsor* is also averted at the last minute, this time because Mine Host of the Garter has contrived to send the potential duellists to different locations. Justice Shallow, another pantaloon, uses the occasion to bore everyone with his own skill as a duellist:

PAGE   *I have heard the Frenchman hath good skill in his rapier.*
SHALLOW *Tut, sir, I could have told you more. In these times you stand on distance, your passes, stoccadoes, and I know not what. 'Tis the heart, Master Page; 'tis here, 'tis here. I have seen the time, with my long sword, I would have made you four tall fellows skip like rats.*

                                           (II. i. 204–11)

He tries to keep up this pretence by claiming that his 'finger itches' (II. iii. 41) every time he watches a duel. Perhaps Antonio's dry fingers just itch to get his own sword out. If, however, he gets closer to pointing it at Claudio then the scene becomes more farcical. Shallow affects to be an old-fashioned duellist who prefers a long or broadsword to a rapier. He also claims to despise the modern technique based on passes and thrusts, or 'stoccadoes'. Such fencing terminology was a part of the Italianate influence on English society in the 1590s, associated with manuals by Giacomo di Grassi, Vicentio Saviolo and others. Like Shallow, Antonio appears to have little time for these new-fangled methods. The references to Claudio's 'nice fence and his active practice' (V. i. 75) and his 'foining fence' are meant to be unflattering ones. Antonio may be a Sicilian but in this attack on Italianate duelling he is standing up for England and old-fashioned English techniques, as far that is as he is able to stand up at all. The parody is sharply double-edged. Critics who suggest that this scene ought to be played to establish sympathy for the wronged Leonato and his brother, and in more general terms the sombre mood appropriate to the middle sections of the play, tend to forget that it is preceded by a courtroom farce.

There are a number of loose ends in *Much Ado*. The reference at the beginning of the play to Claudio's uncle in Messina is not followed up. Antonio is given a son, who has only a walk-on part. The comic way of playing this would be to make him almost an old man in his own right. The play written by the Friar and stage-managed by Leonato demands that Antonio should have a daughter, whom Claudio has to agree to marry in place of Hero. Given the suspicious, close-knit nature of Messinese society, it is highly unlikely that such a daughter would have escaped notice. Although too much should not be read into what is obviously a mechanically convenient fiction, Claudio's willing acceptance of the fiction nevertheless suggests that he might be as gullible at the end of the play as he is at the beginning of it. The point could be reinforced visually if Antonio's pantaloon characteristics are played up. Further doubt could be cast on the existence of such a marriageable daughter by emphasizing Antonio's old age.

The elaborate, Italianate costumes in *Much Ado* should generate comedy in their own right. More specifically, costume changes can be one of the most effective means of visual humour. The best-known example in Shakespeare's plays is probably Malvolio's entrance in his ridiculous courtly attire in *Twelfth Night*. Ben Jonson also exploited the potential of the costume change in *Every Man Out of His Humour*, which incidentally came into the Lord Chamberlain's Men's repertoire at the same time as *Much Ado*. Briefly, an aspiring courtier, Fungoso, tries to imitate the Frenchified dandy, Monsieur Fastidius Brisk. He gets his tailor to run up a copy of one of his idol's satin suits. By the time this is ready, however, Brisk is 'freshly suited' and setting a new fashion. Fungoso goes off to get this copied but is once again too slow:

FUNGOSO *Uncle, God save you; did you see a gentleman, one Monsieur Brisk? A courtier, he goes in such a suit as I do.*
SOGLIARDO *Here is the gentleman, nephew, but not in such a suit.*
FUNGOSO *Another suit!*

(IV. viii. 100–104)

Predictably, he is unable to recognize Brisk the person because the dandy is his clothes. As implied, Don Pedro is a slightly more restrained version of Brisk. Benedick's appearance changes dramatically when he believes that Beatrice is in love with him. He has his beard shaved off and is dressed in more courtly garb. The audience can respond to this visual joke before

73

Benedick actually announces it with the line 'Gallants, I am not as I have been' (III. ii. 14). Some actors claim that they have to hold this line back until some of the laughter has died down. Don Pedro the dandy casts an expert eye over Benedick's new costume:

> There is no appearance of fancy in him, unless it be a fancy that he hath to strange disguises; as to be a Dutchman today, a Frenchman tomorrow, or in the shape of two countries at once, as, a German from the waist downward, all slops, and a Spaniard from the hip upward, no doublet. Unless he have a fancy to this foolery, as it appears he hath, he is no fool for fancy, as you would have it appear he is.
>
> (III. ii. 29–36)

The criticism is that Benedick has not co-ordinated his costume, but has thrown it together in rather a haphazard fashion.

Fastidius Brisk justifies the importance of clothes by claiming that they take 'possession of your stage at your new play' (II. vi. 48). The reference is a satirical one since it is the costumes rather than the actors which steal the show. Costumes nevertheless had a very important part to play in Elizabethan productions, as is confirmed by the inventory drawn up in March 1598 of those owned by the Admiral's Men. The same was not true for stage props. Lingering modern productions of Shakespeare in which the 'traffic' of the stage takes well over two hours are the inevitable result of bardology. They are also brought about by an over-elaborate, fussy concern for *mise en scène*, or the overall 'look' of the production. The Elizabethans kept hand props and stage props to a minimum: a stool for the Sexton, a staff for Verges, tapers for Don Pedro and Claudio, a painted tree or two to represent the orchard. Modern productions have, by contrast, tended to play *Much Ado* as a period piece. It makes relatively little difference whether the period is the Renaissance itself or more modern ones. The effect is the same: a slowing down of the action so that mood and atmosphere can be established. This is a case where visualization can distort the comedy. *Much Ado About Nothing* is not known as *Much Ado* for nothing. There should be a lot of hustle and bustle on stage. An audience is being let off the hook if it is given time to sit back and cast a leisurely eye over the period fixtures and fittings. Questions about theatricality are not posed because supposedly authentic period decor inevitably nudges a production in the direction of naturalism.

The length of modern productions may also have something to do with the fact that a Shakespearean play is packaged as a discreet and self-contained unit. An evening's entertainment consists of a production of *Much Ado*. Elizabethan audiences were more accustomed to a 'flow' of entertainment in which the play itself was just a part. The other entertainments, particularly at the most popular end of the market, might have included fencing matches or prize fights. Most plays were also usually accompanied by a jig. The normal place for this was at the end of a play, although it could be used as a warm-up routine. The accounts of German travellers such as Paul Hentzner and Thomas Platter confirm that the jig, together with other song-and-dance routines, was an important part of the afternoon's entertainments. It was performed by the leading clown together with some of the other comic actors and should not be confused with the politically and sexually safe versions of Elizabethan folk culture which are sometimes rather quaintly staged today. The jig was rude, lewd and often stuffed with topical satire. It was quite literally a series of running gags, both visual and verbal, as the clowns jigged and jumped around the theatre to a musical accompaniment of the 'boom boom' variety. The jokes and gestures were often explicitly sexual ones: Hamlet refers to Polonius's taste 'for a jig or a tale of bawdry' (II. ii. 498). Movements were acrobatic rather than stylized and involved thrills, spills and tumbling tricks. Christopher Sly expressed a preference for this kind of gambolling about in *The Taming of the Shrew*.

Will Kempe, who created the part of Dogberry, was one of the great exponents of the jig. He described himself as a performer of 'mad jigs and merry jests' and was renowned for his acrobatic leaps. *Singing Simpkin*, one of the most popular jigs in the 1590s, may have been written specifically for him. He certainly established the piece as his own. He recorded how 'multitudes of Londoners' turned out to see him start his famous jig to Norwich and how 'many thousand' of them accompanied him to his first port of call. There is some dramatic licence here, but probably not a great deal. Elizabethan clowns were treated as star performers. They traded on such popularity by introducing their own visual versions of 'extemporall merriment' into their scenes. They were also notoriously hard to get off the stage once they had planted their large shoes on it. Editors of *Much Ado* point out that the text is imprecise about exactly how many members of the Watch there are supposed to be. It is also, as noticed, imprecise about what the comics are meant to be doing at certain points. Such gaps would have been filled on the Elizabethan stage by improvised comic routines which played to the particular strengths of the comic company for that afternoon. Clowns also introduced their own verbal material. One of Tarlton's specialities was offering unfriendly words, and gestures, of advice to restless members of the audience. Hamlet's advice to the Players criticizes such verbal improvisation:

And let those that play your clowns speak no more than is set down for them. For there be of them that will themselves laugh to set on some quantity of barren spectators to laugh too, though in the meantime some necessary question of the play be then to be considered.

(III. ii. 37–42)

It would be dangerous to assume that Kempe's brand of fairground clowning was killed off by such hostile reactions to it. It is true that his place in the Lord Chamberlain's Men was taken by Robert Armin, poached from Lord Chandos's Men, who specialized in court fools rather than earthy clowns. He probably created the parts of Feste in *Twelfth Night*, Touchstone in *As You Like It* and the Fool in *King Lear*. If nothing else, however, the continued popularity of *Much Ado* should warn against taking Hamlet's advice as a funeral oration. Elizabethan comedy is stuffed with verbal wit and wordplay. It also needs to be visualized in terms of raunchy, paunchy, red-nosed, blue comedians like Kempe who introduced their own gags and rounded off performances with song-and-dance routines.

Dogberry

The comic constable was a recognizable stage type. The appropriately named Anthony Dull puts in a bemused appearance in *Love's Labour's Lost*. He does not understand a word of the pompous conversations between Holofernes and Sir Nathaniel, but is still able to stump them with a rustic riddle. He mistakes or gets his words jumbled up. The Elizabethans referred to this as misplacing words. The play as a whole suggests that supposedly wiser men than him suffer from the same affliction. Comic misplacement seems to have been one of the obvious characteristics of the stage constable. Elbow has difficulties finding the right word in *Measure for Measure*. Although Dogberry makes some random slips of the tongue, his choice of language usually offers a parody version of correct usage. He opens the trial scene with the words 'Is our whole dissembly appeared?' (IV. ii. 1) This is an attempt to strike a suitably solemn note at the beginning of the proceedings. Dogberry often dresses up his speech in the borrowed robes, or gowns, of legal rhetoric. More specifically, he might be trying here to imitate courtly modes of address. Don Pedro, for instance, greets everybody just before the finale with 'Good morrow to this fair assembly' (V. iv. 34). Dogberry's misplacement of 'assembly' and 'dissembly' is not, however, a completely innocent one. A 'dissembly' is quite literally an appearance or illusion, often associated with theatrical ones. Lady Anne in *Richard III* describes the play-acting Richard as being a 'dissembler' (I. ii. 184). Leonato uses the same term to describe Claudio, implying that his emotions and feelings are merely a counterfeited appearance. Borachio and Conrade are dissemblers in the sense that they have both been involved with a theatrical production. Dogberry's slip of the tongue is thus part of the burlesque version of transgression and redemption, for the dissemblers are to be tried by a dissembly. A theatrical production is to be tried in a theatre of law with Dogberry trying to put in a suitably solemn and dignified performance. The point is underlined a few lines later when Verges claims that he and Dogberry 'have the exhibition to examine' (IV. ii. 5–6). He misplaces commission and 'exhibition' but, once again, the slip is neither random nor innocent. They are, after all, examining an 'exhibition' or theatrical production and, what is more, making an 'exhibition' of themselves in doing so.

The misplacements are not quite so heavily layered with meanings when Dogberry and Verges take their leave of Leonato after comic redemption has triumphed. Dogberry calls the Governor a 'reverend youth' (V. i. 102) and asks God to restore him to health. Leonato may be a 'reverend' and respected member of the community, but both he and Don Pedro have also been playing the parts of irresponsible youths or overgrown schoolboys. So the misplacement, far from being totally confusing, still offers a quite acceptable commentary on events. Dogberry's mistaking of age for youth on this particular occasion is in fact the end of a running gag. When he tries to break the news of the arrest to Leonato, he is immediately sidetracked into an explanation of Verges's shortcomings:

Goodman Verges, sir, speaks a little off the matter – an old man, sir, and his wits are not so blunt as, God help, I would desire they were; but, in faith, honest as the skin between his brows.

(III. v. 9–12)

The comedy works on two levels here. First of all, Dogberry is more prone to speaking 'off the matter' than his companion is. Indeed, this is just what he is doing. Secondly, he is tactless enough to make these remarks to the aged Leonato, whom Benedick describes earlier on as a 'white-bearded fellow' (II. iii. 121). Dogberry thus bemoans the deficiencies of old age to the aged, but provides a graphic illustration of them. These comic points are underlined by the fact that it is Verges, rather than Dogberry, who manages to give the news of the arrest in a straightforward manner. Dogberry leaps in, however, to carry on the running gag:

A good old man, sir, he will be talking; as they say, 'When the age is in, the wit is out.' God help us, it is a world to see! Well said, i'faith, neighbour Verges; well, God's a good man; an two men ride of a horse, one must ride behind. An honest soul, i'faith, sir, by my troth he is, as ever broke bread. But God is to be worshipped; all men are not alike. Alas, good neighbour!

(III. v. 32–8)

It is, however, Dogberry himself who indulges in the kind of witless banter he describes and so ends up patronizing himself.

Even when Dogberry gets things more or less right, his problems are not over. For he tends to set up, unwittingly, the possibilities for alternative readings. He tries to explain the Watch's duties to them:

DOGBERRY   *You are thought here to be the most senseless and fit man for the constable of the watch; therefore bear you the lantern. This is your charge: you shall comprehend all vagrom men; you are to bid any man stand, in the Prince's name.*

SECOND WATCHMAN *How if 'a will not stand?*

DOGBERRY   *Why, then, take no note of him, but let him go; and presently call the rest of the watch together and thank God you are rid of a knave.*

(III. iii. 21–30)

A stand was familiar Elizabethan slanguage for a male erection. So Dogberry is, unintentionally, ordering the Watch to go around telling men to have erections and, what's more, that this is government policy. He is also offering a comic variation on the play's title: sex may be much ado about nothing if a man fails to stand as there will be 'no thing' to 'note'. The humour, such as it is, comes from the fact that it is Dogberry, householder and pillar of the community, who provides the audience with this opportunity for coarse laughter. The single joke, once again, gets incorporated into a running gag:

FIRST WATCHMAN   *We charge you, in the Prince's name, stand!*

SECOND WATCHMAN *Call up the right Master Constable. We have here recovered the most dangerous piece of lechery that ever was known in the commonwealth.*

(III. iii. 158–62)

The misplacement of 'lechery' and treachery confirms the alternative reading. A stand may well be a 'most dangerous piece of lechery'. Borachio and Margaret have also just been performing a 'most dangerous piece of lechery' by pretending to be Hero and her lover.

Shakespeare frequently satirized both the insolence and indolence of legal office, perhaps most notably in *King Lear* and *Measure for Measure*. The indolence of office becomes, in the 'comic climate' of *Much Ado*, a subject for visual and verbal humour. Dogberry and his lazy, crazy gang go out of their way to be as inoffensive as possible. This is an inversion of the constable's role, which was to catch other people for committing offences. Shakespeare then playfully inverts the inversion. The Watch, who appear not to be able to catch a cold or trap a bag of cement, make an important arrest. The 'shallow fools' (V. i. 222) are allowed to outwit the witty courtiers. Similarly, although Dogberry attempts to invert all the principles of justice during the trial, the inversion is itself inverted so that comic justice is done. His misplaced language takes on a special significance in the courtroom. Lawyers pride themselves on being precise, concise and very much to the point. Dogberry, who prides himself on his own elevated part in the proceedings, nevertheless burlesques this tradition. Similarly, legal documentation has a reputation for being pedantically accurate. Most of what Dogberry asks to be taken down falls into the category of utterly useless information. His social snobbery leads him to question the most important piece of information:

DOGBERRY   *... let the watch come forth. Masters, I charge you in the Prince's name, accuse these men.*

FIRST WATCHMAN *This man said, sir, that Don John, the Prince's brother, was a villain.*

DOGBERRY   *Write down Prince John a villain. Why, this is flat perjury, to call a Prince's brother villain.*

(IV. ii. 34–40)

He then allows his disappointment at the fact that the Sexton is no longer present to write down that he is an 'ass' to reach mock-epic proportions. It has no bearing on the case against Conrade and Borachio whether he has been called an 'ass'. He makes one of himself by believing that it does. Ironically, Dogberry feels that his own character is being put on trial. The prosecutor feels that he has to start defending himself:

I am a wise fellow, and, which is more, an officer; and which is more, a householder; and, which is more, as pretty a piece of flesh as any is in Messina; and one that knows the law, go to; and a rich fellow enough, go to; and a fellow that hath had losses; and one that hath two gowns and everything handsome about him.

(IV. ii. 77–83)

Dogberry makes even more of an 'ass' of himself by this inversion of the roles of prosecutor and defendant. Yet the trial scene as a whole at least carries the suggestion that his misplacements, this time of legal theory and practice, may once again be not as wide of the mark as they might appear to be. He has no truck with the belief that people are innocent until proved

79

guilty. After he has got the accuseds' names straight, he informs them that they have already been proved guilty:

Masters, it is proved already that you are little better than false knaves, and it will go near to be thought so shortly. How answer you for yourselves?

(IV. ii. 20–23)

It may be convenient to explain this in terms of comic inversion, but it is important to notice that inversion is also meant to highlight the shortcomings of orthodox behaviour. Don Pedro and Claudio are not that different from Dogberry when they make their plans to shame Hero even before they have seen Don John's evidence:

CLAUDIO   *If I see any thing tonight why I should not marry her,*
           tomorrow in the congregation, where I should wed, there will
           I shame her.
DON PEDRO *And, as I wooed for thee to obtain her, I will join with thee to*
           disgrace her.

(III. ii. 111–15)

Hero is guilty until she can prove herself innocent. Similarly, in the denunciation scene which, point counterpoint, comes immediately before Dogberry's comic legal turns, she is not given the benefit of any doubt. She denies the accusation, parts of which are based on the flimsiest of hearsay evidence, but is nevertheless deemed to be guilty. When Dogberry speaks 'a little off the matter' he often gets uncomfortably close to the truth of it.

It is possible that during his lingering exit Dogberry slaughters that most sacred of sacred cows, the incorruptibility of justice. He has been given his cue to leave, but his sense of his own importance will not allow him to do so. He hangs around on-stage pursuing the red herring about 'one Deformed':

LEONATO   *I thank thee for thy care and honest pains.*
DOGBERRY   *Your worship speaks like a most thankful and reverend youth,*
           and I praise God for you.
LEONATO   *There's for thy pains.*
DOGBERRY   *God save the foundation!*
LEONATO   *Go, I discharge thee of thy prisoner, and I thank thee.*
DOGBERRY   *I leave an arrant knave with your worship; which I beseech*
           your worship to correct yourself, for the example of others.
           God keep your worship! I wish your worship well; God restore

you to health! I humbly give you leave to depart; and if a merry
meeting may be wished, God prohibit it! Come, neighbour.

(V. i. 300–312)

There are a number of ways of playing this exchange. First of all, Dogberry
could be hanging around to indicate, with his hand outstretched, that he
has not been sufficiently rewarded. Leonato gives him the money rather
begrudgingly – 'There's for thy pains' – and he transfers it to the back
pocket. Such an interpretation would point up the burlesque of justice:
the redeemer, like the transgressor, acts out of selfish motives. Secondly,
the concentration could be on Leonato. Far from being tetchy, he might
now have recovered some of the liberality and largesse that characterized
him in the early scenes. Thirdly, it could be played in a more stylized and
theatrical manner. Clowns were notoriously difficult to get off the stage,
particularly when the audience was warmed up. Dogberry's lingering
farewell might thus be a parody, which is also a self-parody, of this fact
of theatrical life. If so, then it provides another example of the way in
which *Much Ado* draws attention to its own theatricality.

6 Hero and Claudio

Feminine silence

Don John's relative silence during the welcoming ceremonies is neatly paralleled by that of Hero: both villain and victim are unaccustomed to public speaking. Hero's silence is, however, golden and virtuous as it clearly marks her out as the modest, dutiful daughter. She tends to speak only when spoken to. Leonato's question about the identity of one Signor Mountanto is probably addressed to Beatrice. Hero nevertheless decides to answer it, sensing perhaps that her father will not get a straight answer from Beatrice: 'My cousin means Signor Benedick of Padua' (I. i. 33). She is on stage throughout the banter with the Messenger and the welcome for the heroes, but this is her only verbal contribution to the proceedings. She is expected to make her contribution in other ways, being very much the object of the visual and verbal attentions of the new male guests. She is talked about and talked at, but not expected to reply. The tone of these exchanges can be offensive:

DON PEDRO *I think this is your daughter.*
LEONATO *Her mother hath many times told me so.*
BENEDICK *Were you in doubt, sir, that you asked her?*
LEONATO *Signor Benedick, no; for then were you a child.*
DON PEDRO *You have it full, Benedick; we may guess by this what you are, being a man. Truly, the lady fathers herself. Be happy, lady; for you are like an honourable father.*

(I. i. 96–104)

Don Pedro, the model of courtesy, pays the unmarried Hero the highest compliment. Leonato, trying to engage in courtly wit, manages to be less complimentary. Hero's passivity is conditioned by the fact that there are no independent activities, and therefore set of responses, which she can cultivate. Daughters were expected, in Brabantio's words in *Othello*, to be 'still and quiet' (I. iii. 95). Hero does not draw attention to herself verbally and it has to be assumed that her stage presence ought to be passive and undemonstrative. Beatrice's reference to Hero making 'curtsy' (II. i. 47) to Leonato suggests one way in which her gestures could be made to reinforce her submissiveness. It was a common practice in Renaissance households for members of the family, together with the servants, to 'make curtsy' every day at quite a formal ceremony in front of the head of the family.

Hero makes her second brief response just before the masked ball. The talk is of Don John's absence and she points out that he is 'of a very melancholy disposition (II. i. 5). She contributes to a conversation, albeit very briefly, but does not initiate it. It seems likely that on this occasion her statement of the obvious is directed at Beatrice rather than at Leonato or Antonio. She proves later on in the play that she is more at ease in female, as opposed to mixed, company. The purpose of this family conference before the masked ball is to prepare her to play her part correctly when Don Pedro makes his move. Antonio has already warned her, off-stage, what might happen. He tells her now that she ought to 'be ruled by your father' (II. i. 44–5), but receives no reply. None is perhaps necessary. She also has no response to make when her father tells her what to do:

Daughter, remember what I told you. If the Prince do solicit you in that kind, you know your answer.

(II. i. 58 60)

Hero's answers are not her own to give. Leonato's tone here is both assured and mild. There can be no clearer indication during the denunciation scene that he has lost faith in his daughter than when he actually charges her on her filial duty to tell the truth. As Hero is conditioned to dutiful silence, it is doubtful whether she is being upstaged by Beatrice during this conference. Beatrice steals the scene, but not necessarily from her. Here and elsewhere, her extreme reticence is drawn attention to by Beatrice's extreme volubility, and of course vice versa. Such extremities are in keeping with the play's 'comic climate'.

It would be dangerous to see this extreme polarity as a case of the conventional, passive heroine being shown up by a more unconventional, active one. Beatrice's role as the fast-talking, disdainful lady is an equally conventional one. So much so that at one point Don Pedro declares that her 'silence most offends' (II. i. 306) him, meaning also that it would offend against convention. Beatrice does not have a father to rule her and she is also older than Hero, so she is accorded more independence than her cousin. The important point, however, is that such independence is still governed by convention. Beatrice and Hero both have parts to act for their male audiences: the one to amuse and abuse with her wit, the other to gratify with her presence. *Much Ado* contains a number of double acts, for instance Dogberry and Verges, Don Pedro and Claudio, Beatrice herself and Benedick. Beatrice and Hero function more as a cross-talk act in which one of the members takes the initiative. There are important differences between their act and that staged by Kate and Bianca in *The Taming of the Shrew* and, as indicated, that staged by Lady Emilia and Duchess Elizabetta in *The Courtier*. Yet the overall pattern of the relationships is the same.

Contemporary feminist criticism suggests that a woman's silence can be interpreted as a positive, and in some cases a radical, statement. It might question the categories that have just been used: Hero as passive and Beatrice as active. At its most radical, the argument points out that women, by withdrawing from the confines of a 'man-made language', are liberating themselves from perhaps the most insidious form of repression. Some Shakespearean heroines, whilst not withdrawing completely, nevertheless use the positive or deafening silence very effectively. Cordelia in *King Lear* signals her distaste for the rhetorical games her father expects her to play with the brief reply of 'Nothing' (I. i. 89). Hero's relative silence during the denunciation scene is open to a positive interpretation. It would be dangerous, however, to try to incorporate her earlier performances into such a pattern.

Hero reveals, when she does speak, that she is perfectly content with the part that male Messinese society expects her to play. The first example comes when Don Pedro is planning his plays to gull Beatrice and Benedick:

DON PEDRO *I would fain have it a match, and I doubt not but to fashion it, if you three will but minister such assistance as I shall give you direction.*

LEONATO *My lord, I am for you, though it cost me ten nights' watchings.*

CLAUDIO *And I, my lord.*

DON PEDRO *And you too, gentle Hero?*

HERO *I will do any modest office, my lord, to help my cousin to a good husband.*

(II. i. 340–48)

Hero's reply, unlike those of her father and future husband, has to be solicited. When it comes, however, it reveals complete acceptance of her role. The implication of her statement is that both the function and reward of feminine 'modesty' can be related to a 'good husband'.

Hero reveals briefly another side during the masked ball. The dance is, incidentally, a pavane in which the couples move at walking pace, turning, retreating and then advancing towards each other. She engages in some witty banter with Don Pedro: 'God defend the lute should be like the case' (II. i. 84–5). She also lets him know, again in a witty way, that she has seen through his disguise:

DON PEDRO *My visor is Philemon's roof; within the house is Jove.*
HERO   *Why, then, your visor should be thatched.*

                                          (II. i. 86–7)

Editors can make rather heavy weather of this exchange by going back to
Ovid to nail the allusion. At a more prosaic level, Hero is telling Don
Pedro that his balding head gives the game away. It is perfectly acceptable
for her to backchat the Prince in this way as the conventions of the
masquerade give her the licence to do so. It is one of the few occasions in
mixed company where she is expected to be witty as well as pretty.
The use of disguise and the festive atmosphere allow for a temporary
suspension of the more rigid social conventions. Romeo and Juliet, for
instance, are able to begin their relationship only because they do so at a
masked ball.

Hero's parts

Hero's playfulness becomes more apparent during the gulling of Beatrice.
She is acting here within her own 'sphere': there are no men present and
her two accomplices are Margaret and Ursula. Given the cast, however,
she is still on a form of public stage. In general, Renaissance women do
not seem to have regarded privacy, a room of their own, as a positive goal.
Hero shares a room with Beatrice except for the night before her wedding.
She takes it upon herself to play the leading lady in the play that is acted
out for her cousin's benefit. A good deal of *Much Ado* is written in
either formal or conversational prose. She decides that these are totally
inappropriate for such a theatrical moment. Even before Beatrice is
in position, she is running through her repertoire of fine-sounding, if
somewhat clichéd, metaphors:

> say that thou overheardst us,
> And bid her steal into the pleachèd bower,
> Where honeysuckles, ripened by the sun,
> Forbid the sun to enter – like favourites,
> Made proud by princes, that advance their pride
> Against that power that bred it. There will she hide her,
> To listen our propose. This is thy office;
> Bear thee well in it, and leave us alone.

                                          (III. i. 6–13)

Hero is too conscious of giving a performance, both to her maids and
later to Beatrice. She strives a little too hard for effect: the metaphor about

the court favourites is gratuitous and redundant. Dogberry is not the only character whose language gives rise to comedy. It is significant that, after two acts of relative silence, Hero's language should be revealed as a borrowed, and in some cases badly fitting, one. Speech, like clothes, can be an attempt at fashionable disguise. As all Elizabethan language can seem rather elaborate and ornate, it is important to stress that part of the comedy in this scene comes from the fact that the inexperienced Hero is shown to be such a long-winded actress:

> *Why, you speak truth. I never yet saw man,*
> *How wise, how noble, young, how rarely featured,*
> *But she would spell him backward. If fair-faced,*
> *She would swear the gentleman should be her sister;*
> *If black, why, Nature, drawing of an antic,*
> *Made a foul blot; if tall, a lance ill-headed;*
> *If low, an agate very vilely cut;*
> *If speaking, why, a vane blown with all winds;*
> *If silent, why, a block movèd with none.*
> *So turns she every man the wrong side out,*
> *And never gives to truth and virtue that*
> *Which simpleness and merit purchaseth.*

(III. i. 59–70)

If nothing else, as Hero herself might put it, the repetition of 'why' ought to have made Beatrice ask why on earth her cousin, normally so reticent, was behaving in this gushing, theatrical manner. Don John, the man of few words, finds a torrent of them when he is alone with Conrade. Hero, the woman of few words, also finds more than she can use convincingly when she addresses her maid. Although, as suggested, this can be explained logically, its comic explanation lies in the humour that attaches itself to a sudden reversal. Besides using the occasion to indulge her raw theatrical talents, Hero also uses it to pass on some helpful hints. She tells Beatrice not just how to get a 'good husband' but how to keep him as well. Her recipe for a happy home is to banish female 'disdain and scorn' (III. i. 51) from it. She and Ursula then exit to try on wedding dresses, leaving Beatrice to take this advice to heart. The fact that the older, supposedly more perceptive woman falls completely for these amateur dramatics intensifies the comedy of the scene.

Hero and Ursula do not reach a decision about the wedding dress now. There are still some doubts about it on the wedding day itself. The tendency for criticism of *Much Ado* to confine itself to certain supposedly high points in the play – the denunciation, Beatrice's command to

Benedick to 'Kill Claudio' and Claudio's repentance at Hero's tomb – has meant that the scene in which Hero prepares herself for the wedding has not received the attention it deserves. If it is dealt with at all, it is usually in terms of building up sympathy for a nice, ordinary Hero. It is, thankfully, a lot more interesting than this. There are two ways of playing the scene. The first is to do it with due deference to Hero's modesty, which receives further confirmation during the scene itself. She is thus shown to be nearly fully dressed from the beginning and the action revolves around the addition of last-minute accessories. Her cry at the end – 'Help to dress me, good coz, good Meg, good Ursula' (III. iv. 89–90) thus becomes more of a general signal of panic than a specific command. The second way is to have Hero virtually undressed at the beginning and then trying on parts of her wardrobe in the sense of holding them up against her. She is probably only half-dressed by the end of the scene so that her command is a genuine one. This second interpretation seems more appropriate, particularly as physical as opposed to verbal modesty is not really an issue in this single-sex environment. All audiences are eavesdroppers. *Much Ado* self-consciously draws attention to this by making overheard conversations such a central part of the plot. All audiences, almost by definition, are also voyeurs. Once again, the relationship between audience and play, spectator and spectacle, is self-consciously drawn attention to, particularly in this scene which involves the rituals of dressing with perhaps some undressing thrown in for good measure. No audience has a single or uniform perception of a play. At its most obvious, different vantage points within the theatre will produce different views and points of view. At a more complicated level, different class and gender vantage points will also produce different views and points of view. Matters are complicated still further by the fact that Shakespearean comedy usually plays in and around the whole notion of multiple perception and reception. It is still probably true, that modern performances of this scene are at least inviting male members of the audience to look on and gaze at Hero in much the same way as Claudio does. The invitation is to agree or disagree with his statement that 'In mine eye she is the sweetest lady that ever I looked on' (I. i. 75–6). The voyeurs in the audience are in a more privileged position than Claudio, the voyeur on stage. The view of Hero that is being displayed is one to which Claudio is not given access. In more general terms, all sections of the audience know, or ought to know, a great deal more about what is happening than any of the participants do. This paradoxically encourages them to participate in the action, whilst also underlining their essentially passive role. This scene serves to heighten such theatricality by offering a privileged but passive or voyeuristic perspective to the theatre audience.

The scene is usually set either in a bedroom or a more neutral dressing room. At one level, it shows Hero making ready for her wedding. At another level, it shows an actress making up and dressing up to play a part. Although it is played on-stage, it once again emphasizes theatricality by drawing attention to the artificiality of performance. For the true location is the theatrical dressing room, usually a secret place that is jealously withheld from an audience but is here displayed for all to see. As suggested earlier, Shakespeare reveals illusion not to destroy it but to sustain it. An Elizabethan audience would have seen a boy preparing to play the part of a girl, so both the sense of revelation and the consciousness of theatricality which accompanies it would have been even greater. This scene, far from soliciting a sympathetic identification with a 'character' called Hero, would have left no doubt that there was just a 'part' called Hero which was played by a boy. Interestingly, there is a broadly similar revelation at the beginning of *The Taming of the Shrew*, during what is known as the Induction. This opens with Christopher Sly, a tinker, being kicked out of the pub and settling down to sleep the sleep of the just plain drunk. A Lord and his servants, who are out hunting, decide to play a practical joke on him. They take him back to their country house and dress him up as a nobleman. They then try to persuade him to accept this theatrical illusion as the reality. Meanwhile, some travelling players arrive and prepare to stage their own play about Petruchio and Katherina. The Lord instructs one of his servants to get his page, Bartholomew, ready to play the part of Sly's wife:

> *Such duty to the drunkard let him do,*
> *With soft low tongue and lowly courtesy,*
> *And say 'What is't your honour will command,*
> *Wherein your lady and your humble wife*
> *May show her duty and make known her love?'*
> *And then with kind embracements, tempting kisses,*
> *And with declining head into his bosom,*
> *Bid him shed tears, as being overjoyed*
> *To see her noble lord restored to health,*
> *Who for this seven years hath esteemèd him*
> *No better than a poor and loathsome beggar.*
>
> (111–21)

The page, dressed as a woman, has a brief, flirtatious reunion with Sly and then they sit back to watch the play about Padua. The kaleidoscopic effect of placing this within the play to gull Sly is to underline its theatricality. Similarly, the explicit references to women's parts being played by male actors draw attention to the artificiality of performance.

The denunciation scene represents the most heightened piece of drama in a play which revels in performance and performances. The revelation of the actor who is going to play Hero getting ready for the part would have left Elizabethan audiences in no doubt that they were being asked to judge performance as performance. The modern critical and theatrical tendency to sentimentalize Hero's denunciation, to see her as an innocent 'character' and her accusers as cruel 'characters', or even people, entirely misses the point of the play. Claudio's charge, unspecified in the early stages of the proceedings, is that Hero is not a maid or virgin:

> *Behold how like a maid she blushes here!*
> *O, what authority and show of truth*
> *Can cunning sin cover itself withal!*
> *Comes not that blood as modest evidence*
> *To witness simple virtue? Would you not swear,*
> *All you that see her, that she were a maid*
> *By these exterior shows?*
>
> (IV. i. 32–8)

The permutations that were available to an Elizabethan audience are almost too complicated to be reconstructed. Everyone would have known that she was not a maid and they would have seen the 'exterior shows' which were used to create this 'show of truth'. Claudio's rhetorical question is addressed to the theatre as well as the stage audience. Elizabethan responses, far from being conditioned by sympathy for Hero, would have been influenced by the irony and ambiguity, some of it sexual, which Claudio's outburst generates. A limited amount of this irony is still available to a modern audience. Claudio accuses Hero of being a skilled actress, whereas all the evidence to date suggests that she is an appalling one. Claudio, who claims to be able to strip away the illusion to find the reality, is giving a very self-conscious performance motivated entirely by illusion. For Elizabethan audiences, the comedy might have continued right up to the last scene when Hero announces that 'And surely as I live, I am a maid' (V. iv. 64). The finale, far from being a logical separation of illusion from reality, might have been interpreted as the triumph of illusion over reality.

Claudio as mock-heroic part

The Messenger provides Claudio with a star billing:

> He hath borne himself beyond the promise of his age, doing, in the figure of a lamb, the feats of a lion; he hath indeed better bettered expectation than you must expect of me to tell you how.

> (I. i. 13–16)

The 'comic climate' of *Much Ado* is established immediately by this Messenger who is incapable of delivering a simple message. This mock-heroic tone demands that Claudio always has to play the lamb. He is conspicuous by his silent presence during the round of welcoming speeches. Although Leonato appears to know both him and his family, he is not drawn into the festive circle. Perhaps the lamb-like hero is so shy and retiring that he is not even noticed. When Leonato and Don Pedro hold their private conference, the stage is dominated by Beatrice and Benedick. Claudio is quite content to provide part of the on-stage audience for their skirmish of wit. Other members of this audience are Hero, Balthasar, possibly Don John and some attendant lords to swell out the scene. The grouping and positioning for this very self-conscious play within the play needs to be quite carefully arranged. Claudio has to be in a position to look at Hero but, as implied earlier on, the theatre audience need to be able to follow his eye-line to her.

Claudio's first words, again in keeping with the mock-heroic tone, are tentative and possibly even bashful. He asks Benedick whether he has noted 'the daughter of Signor Leonato' (I. i. 152–3). Claudio reveals a little later on that he knows her name. There are, indeed, very few secrets in this suspicious, tightly knit society. He may not use it on this occasion either because he wants to appear correct, or else just because he is a little afraid to do so. He is doing in the figure of a lamb the feats of a lamb now that he has left the battlefield. Benedick makes the most of his younger friend's inexperience. Claudio asks him to speak in 'sober judgement' (I. i. 160), but receives some intoxicated wordplay. For Benedick, the truth is just another part to be played. He asks Claudio to be more explicit, or professional, about what part he himself is playing. The implication being that it is difficult to play the game unless one knows what the rules are:

> But speak you this with a sad brow? Or do you play the flouting Jack, to tell us Cupid is a good hare-finder, and Vulcan a rare carpenter? Come, in what key shall a man take you to go in the song?

> (I. i. 170–74)

Like Benedick, most critics have been unsure about Claudio's 'key' and have therefore transformed him into a problem character in a problem play. The solution might well be to suggest that Claudio himself does not know what key to strike. He is unsure of which part to play and how to play any of them. He is also unable to spot what parts other people might be playing. It is not too difficult for him in this exchange to work out that Benedick is 'in sport', but Don Pedro presents him with more of a problem:

CLAUDIO	*If this were so, so were it uttered.*
BENEDICK	*Like the old tale, my lord: 'It is not so, nor 'twas not so; but, indeed, God forbid it should be so!'*
CLAUDIO	*If my passion change not shortly, God forbid it should be otherwise!*
DON PEDRO	*Amen, if you love her; for the lady is very well worthy.*
CLAUDIO	*You speak this to fetch me in, my lord.*
DON PEDRO	*By my troth, I speak my thought.*
CLAUDIO	*And in faith, my lord, I spoke mine.*

(I. i. 199–208)

Claudio's final comment is ironic since this is exactly what he has not been doing. His questions and responses to both Don Pedro and Benedick have been evasive and cryptic up to this point. He covers a lot of options with the conditional statement 'If my passion change not shortly, God forbid it should be otherwise'. Don Pedro and Benedick are running rings around him. He is genuinely unsure whether Don Pedro is playing the part of an honest man or whether he is trying to 'fetch him in'.

Claudio is a bit more comfortable when the flouting, jesting Benedick exits. Critics who support the arranged marriage thesis make much ado of his question to Don Pedro: 'Hath Leonato any son, my lord?' (I. i. 273). The suggestion is made that he is more interested in money than love. His eye is not really for Hero but for the main chance. The question is, however, perfectly in keeping with his awkward and indirect way of approaching the subject of Hero. Claudio the soldier is not very accomplished at playing other parts. Incidentally, his reputation as a soldier rests on the testimony of the Messenger and Benedick, neither of whom are particularly reliable witnesses. There are two subsidiary arguments against the arranged marriage interpretation. First, Claudio is not alone in making a natural equation between marriage and inheritance. Leonato represents the fictitious daughter of Antonio as an heiress as if it were perfectly normal for Claudio's financial prospects to be considered briefly. Secondly, Hero may not have been the most attractive match from a purely mercenary point of view. Count Claudio, the intimate friend of Prince Don Pedro, could probably have set his sights a little higher. His indirect questions and conditional statements betray, not indifference to Hero, but an inability to trust his own judgement. He is unwilling to take the romantic plunge until both Benedick and Don Pedro have indicated their support. He is particularly concerned to guard himself against the charge of acting rashly. If he is seen as fumbling his way into the part of the romantic lover, then his choice of language is often ironically inappropriate. He speaks of, and sometimes with, 'sober judgement', which was exactly the quality that any half-decent lover would cast aside. Beatrice provides an important clue to Claudio's contradictory approach to love just before the betrothal when she describes him as 'civil':

The Count is neither sad, not sick, nor merry, nor well; but civil count, civil as an orange, and something of that jealous complexion.

(II. i. 269–71)

As suggested by the equation of civility and jealousy, it is possible that Claudio uses a prosaic, civil discourse to mask his emotions. This protective mask also helps him to overcome his awkwardness at playing new parts.

The ease with which Claudio falls for Don John's first plot illustrates, once again, that he has difficulties in working out whether he is being fetched in or not. He is obviously not alone in this, although the point is made here with deft irony. Claudio wears a mask but is gullible, whereas Don John does not wear a disguise but is being devious. The incident also sustains the mock-heroic tone. Don John may be a bit slow, although even he is able to run rings around Claudio. Claudio, valiant trooper and man of action, fails to recognize his enemy. The defeated Don John wins an easy victory over the triumphant Claudio, who goes into a sulk and delivers a wooden little soliloquy on how male friendship is destroyed by love. It would, in performance, be possible to emphasize his gullibility by overstating some of Don Pedro's camp mannerisms and gestures. An audience could then be left in little doubt about the older man's strictly honourable intentions towards Hero. Claudio's petulant performance is . shown to be much ado about nothing when Don Pedro reveals that honour has indeed been the name of his little game with Hero. The two young lovers are both awkward and bashful:

LEONATO   *Count, take of me my daughter, and with her my fortunes. His grace hath made the match, and all Grace say Amen to it!*
BEATRICE   *Speak, Count, 'tis your cue.*
CLAUDIO   *Silence is the perfectest herald of joy; I were but little happy, if I could say how much. Lady, as you are mine, I am yours; I give away myself for you and dote upon the exchange.*

BEATRICE *Speak, cousin; or, if you cannot, stop his mouth with a kiss, and let not him speak neither.*

(II. i. 278–87)

Beatrice, true to form, is probably leaping in just a little bit too quickly to cue and prompt Claudio and Hero. She is the accomplished actress who, playfully, suggests that other members of the ensemble are a bit slow on the uptake. Claudio, perhaps unwittingly, ties himself up in paradoxes but Hero, also true to form, remains silent. Beatrice, the stage-manager and prompter, now supplies a running commentary on Hero's more private responses: 'My cousin tells him in his ear that he is in her heart' (II. i. 290–91). This may be wishful, or playful, thinking on Beatrice's part.

Double acts

The opening scenes of the play set up an interesting and potentially comic opposition between those who make much ado of speaking and those who appear to have nothing to say. Beatrice, Benedick, Leonato and Don Pedro obviously fall into the first category. Claudio, Hero and, to a lesser extent Don John, fall into the second category, although they all do so for markedly different reasons. Claudio's performances early on in the play are embarrassingly bad. He takes upon himself the part of juvenile lead, but does not have the capacity to play it. He is too inexperienced to undertake the big parts just yet. He is, nevertheless, quite good, as might be expected, as a stooge in double acts and ensembles where he knows the responses. Leonato fumbles his lines on at least one occasion during the gulling of Benedick, but Claudio demonstrates good reactions and reflexes. As well as participating in this play with Leonato and Don Pedro, he is agile enough to note how it is being received by its on-stage audience. It is only, when all is said and done, a part in a short comedy three-hander, but that might be the limit of the young Claudio's theatrical abilities. The suggestion, which is being made throughout this particular reading of the play, that *Much Ado* draws attention to its own theatricality, should not be taken to imply that just one style of acting or type of theatre is being self-consciously revealed. Accomplished actors take the stage alongside novices. Big set-pieces like the denunciation scene are framed by comedy turns and routines. A few critics have found this range and diversity so bewildering that they have suggested that *Much Ado* is a problem play because it lacks unity. This view does not need to be taken seriously. At a thematic level, it can be shown that *Much Ado* plays a number of skilful variations on basic themes. The way it does so through a variety of different theatrical modes might still seem to be rather confusing, although the unity is provided by the exposure of theatricality in all its diversity. These remarks represent a complicated way of introducing a very simple point, so simple in fact that it is rarely noticed. The gulling of Benedick takes a particular theatrical form, namely that of the improvisation. It is the kind of dramatic game that might be played in any drama class or studio: three actors have to improvise a play to persuade somebody that he ought to love rather than hate an old enemy. It is what the Elizabethans would have called a 'play extempore'. *Much Ado* is full of polished and over-polished performances. The edges are a bit rougher here, for instance the occasion when Leonato fluffs his part and has to be rescued:

DON PEDRO *Why, what effects of passion shows she?*

CLAUDIO *Bait the hook well; this fish will bite.*

LEONATO *What effects, my lord? She will sit you – you heard my daughter tell you how.*

CLAUDIO *She did, indeed.*

DON PEDRO *How, how, I pray you? You amaze me; I would have thought her spirit had been invincible against all assaults of affection.*

LEONATO *I would have sworn it had, my lord, especially against Benedick.*

(II. iii. 109–19)

Elizabethan actors, tragedians as well as comedians, had to have a facility for improvisation, given the large number of parts that had to be learnt. It ought to be emphasized that Shakespeare was an actor as well as a writer. Indeed, it could be argued that only somebody with such experience could write a piece of actor's theatre like *Much Ado*. The Elizabethan theatre was certainly not a director's medium. The prompter or 'book-holder' undertook stage-managerial functions, but the assumption must be that the actors together with the writer, particularly if he was also a member of the company, directed a play. Recent criticism has shown quite successfully that Shakespeare's stage directions can be interpretive rather than purely functional. It is not known, however, whether Shakespeare collaborated with the other actors in the writing of a play. Improvisations such as the garden scenes in *Much Ado* suggest that a certain amount of ensemble writing was a possibility.

The point about theatrical range and diversity is underlined by the way in which both Don Pedro and Claudio are playing well-rehearsed, even over-rehearsed parts during the denunciation scene, rather than improvised ones. They signal their possible intention of shaming Hero in public before they witness Don John's production and, after it, they have enough time to prepare their parts. Given the circumstances, Claudio now has to make most of the theatrical running but the old double-act routines are still capitalized upon:

CLAUDIO   *And what have I to give you back, whose worth*
                May counterpoise this rich and precious gift?
DON PEDRO *Nothing, unless you render her again.*
CLAUDIO   *Sweet Prince, you learn me noble thankfulness.*
                There, Leonato, take her back again, ...

(IV. i. 25–9)

Leonato, Hero and the others are inevitably not prepared for the speed and polish of these rhetorical 'one-two' movements. Don Pedro, bang on cue, feeds Claudio the opportunity to deliver his set piece about rotten oranges and 'exterior shows'. Claudio and Hero should be holding hands at this point, so Claudio literally gives Leonato his daughter 'back again'. The ceremonial gestures of the wedding are turned upside down.

    The perception of all Elizabethan language as elaborate and ornate should not be allowed to obscure the way in which Claudio self-consciously strives for effect during these exchanges:

> *Out on thee! Seeming! I will write against it.*
> *You seem to me as Dian in her orb,*
> *As chaste as is the bud ere it be blown;*
> *But you are more intemperate in your blood*
> *Than Venus, or those pampered animals*
> *That rage in savage sensuality.*

(IV. i. 54–9)

Why does Claudio use 'write' here when he is in fact going to speak against 'seeming'? Editorial explanations and glosses do not provide a satisfactory answer. It may be that his carefully prepared performance is coming unstuck at this point. He knows the lines appropriate for the part of injured innocence better than he did those for the young lover, but there is still some confusion between the written and the spoken part. The muddled sense of the line might be something like 'Stop pretending to be virtuous. I wrote out a few words on exactly this point.' Claudio, like Dogberry, is misplacing his words: his use of 'write' rather than speak should draw attention to the fact that his performance, whilst being a carefully prepared one, is predictably enough not a word-perfect one. He still has difficulty trying to play the leading roles. Other parts of his performance underline its over-elaboration:

> *But fare thee well, most foul, most fair! Farewell,*
> *Thou pure impiety and impious purity!*
>
> (IV. i. 101–2)

The Elizabethans were, of course, fascinated by puns and riddles, but Claudio's lack of spontaneity and facility draw attention to themselves. He has landed himself with a real tongue-twister, which incidentally echoes the final words of his soliloquy after the masked ball, at a completely inappropriate moment in his performance.

The denunciation scene

A number of points remain to be made about this scene. Claudio's charge against Hero, when it becomes more specific, is that she has brought her own name and therefore that of her father into disrepute. He claims, adopting the manner of a religious catechism, that he is going to make her 'answer truly' to her name. It is unlikely that he means that she has sullied the particular name of Hero with its classical associations of constancy if not chastity. He is probably more concerned to suggest that, by bringing her father into disrepute, she has to lose the name that he has given her. In terms quite explicitly suggested by the play's title, he implies that Hero ought to be *nemo*, which can be translated as no name but which also carried the wider meaning of nothing. A person without a name was nothing because they were denied religious, social and legal status. As just noted, the religious catechism involved answering to a name. Hero could also expect to be excluded socially. Don Pedro pointedly refuses to call her by her name until after Borachio's confession. He tells Leonato, rather unconvincingly, during the duelling scene that his heart 'is sorry for your daughter's death' (V. i. 103). He refers to her later on as 'the old man's daughter' (V. i. 171). She could also expect to forfeit her legal rights. This is confirmed in the very next scene when Dogberry makes much ado at the beginning of the trial about getting Borachio and Conrade to 'answer truly' to their names.

As might be expected, Hero is in complete agreement with the way in which male society punishes those who offend against its taboos concerning chastity and legitimacy. She wants her father to reject her, if the charge can be proved. Claudio harangues her father rather than her at the beginning of the denunciation. This confirms the pattern of the earlier scenes in which she was talked about, and occasionally to, but not required to answer. Her responses, when they eventually come, initially take the form of a series of questions, which indicate a refusal to participate in the proceedings. Her modesty obviously prevents her from indulging in a long defence, but the point may be that now her relative silence has a tougher edge. She questions the questioners:

CLAUDIO   *Let me but move one question to your daughter;*
           And, by that fatherly and kindly power
           That you have in her, bid her answer truly.
LEONATO   *I charge thee do so, as thou art my child.*
HERO   *O God defend me! How am I beset!*
           What kind of catechizing call you this?
CLAUDIO   *To make you answer truly to your name.*
HERO   *Is it not Hero? Who can blot that name*
           With any just reproach?

(IV. i. 71–9)

Hero questions the inquisitorial process and her short denial of the accusation itself can, in performance, achieve unexpected eloquence, surrounded as it is by such coarse acting.

Claudio and Leonato are both acting entirely in accordance with Renaissance versions of patriarchy when they insist that Hero should answer to her name. The theory is on their side but, in practice, they are over-reacting and therefore over-acting. Their concern for name becomes an obsession. This represents a variation on the 'fashion is the fashion' theme. Just as costumes can become more important than the person, so a name is more significant than the wearer of it. Leonato draws attention to the way in which Claudio's carefully rehearsed performance is accompanied by stage tears. He himself indulges in histrionic gestures, begging somebody to stab him just before Hero swoons. His impatience during the early stages of the denunciation gives way to anger towards the end. He forgets, rather like Dogberry does, that he is not the defendant. Once again, although both textual and contextual explanations indicate that he does in fact stand accused with his daughter, he nevertheless makes too much ado about how the accusation threatens his own self-important view of himself. His constant repetition of 'mine' shows that, like Claudio, he is unable to see beyond himself. This is ironic since Hero's accusers, with whom Leonato sides, claim to have a privileged vision.

It is therefore left to the Friar to set about clearing Hero's name. He is usually held to be a benign presence who eventually leads the participants out of this selfish darkness into the light of knowledge and self-knowledge. There are, however, a number of problems with such an interpretation. The Friar is not particularly competent. He muddles up the groom and father of the bride at the beginning of the marriage service, which is no mean achievement given Leonato's age. Ironically, he too is one of the play's old men. He also had, as far as Elizabethan audiences were concerned, the dubious distinction of representing Roman Catholicism to a nominally Protestant audience. His Catholicism is played up rather than down. He asks Hero to confess to him so that he can begin the redemptive process. He also decides that it is necessary to be mysterious concerning the true facts of somebody who has, to all intents and purposes, risen from the dead. He believes that this will drive Claudio to do penance for his sins. As friars had a bad press in Elizabethan England for chastity, both his 'noting' of the lady and his attempt to help her might have been open to misinterpretation. The opening words of the confessional – 'Lady, what man is he you are accused of?' (IV. i. 174) – might have confirmed popular prejudices against friars who took an unhealthy interest in the sins of the flesh. The popular jestbook which Benedick accuses Beatrice of plagiarizing, *Hundred Merry Tales*, contains its fair share of 'friar jokes'. The Friar is a redeemer but he may be, like Dogberry, a comic one. The text itself provides less speculative evidence. First of all, he quite simply gets it wrong. His elaborate plot to make Claudio do penance for his sins backfires. Claudio only decides to mourn Hero after Borachio's confession has left no doubt as to what has happened. Secondly, the Friar may genuinely want to help Hero regain her name, but he also wants to establish his own name for sermonizing advice. His misreading of Claudio's responses is set in amongst a string of platitudes:

> *... for it so falls out*
> *That what we have we prize not to the worth*
> *Whiles we enjoy it, but being lacked and lost,*
> *Why, then we rack the value, then we find*
> *The virtue that possession would not show us*
> *Whiles it was ours. So will it fare with Claudio.*
> (IV. i. 215–20)

There is some irony attached to the fact that the Friar, like Leonato, is concerned to establish his own good name.

The Friar and Leonato, prompted by Benedick, eventually join forces to re-establish Hero's name. Don John and Borachio wrote a script to defame her, so these two old men, supported later by Antonio, write one to reverse this process. Both scenarios call for Don Pedro and Claudio to be manipulated. Name and reputation are destroyed by theatrical devices and then restored by them. *Much Ado* does not therefore offer crude distinctions between illusion and reality. It suggests rather a distinction between 'honest slanders' (III. i. 84) and dishonest slanders, honest and dishonest illusions. The denunciation scene represents the apparent triumph of this dishonest illusion. Yet it also sees the groundwork being laid for the eventual victory of honest illusion: Claudio, like Beatrice and Benedick, is tricked into marriage. Tricking into marriage is honest, whereas attempting to deceive out of marriage is dishonest. The dishonest trickster, Don John, is a comic villain and the honest redeemer, Dogberry, a bumbling fool. It is therefore appropriate to the overall pattern of the play that parts at least of the Friar's performance during the denunciation scene should indicate that he is on the side of the bumbling, self-important, comic angels.

The tomb scene

Claudio's repentance at Hero's tomb needs to be visualized. It is obviously not just the slapstick routines and comic turns which benefit from a perspective which encompasses staging and stage presence. Don Pedro and Claudio's change of costume provides a visual indication of change of mood. A stage direction is also contained in the text. Don Pedro suggests that the participants take their leave and 'put on other weeds' (V. iii. 30), or clothes. They have all obviously changed into costumes which are a shade or two more sombre for this particular occasion. The reference also provides a clear reminder of theatricality. Don Pedro and Claudio, together with Balthasar and the attendant lords, are acting parts that have been created for them by the Friar and Leonato. This sombre mood is enhanced by music, which would have been particularly important on the Elizabethan stage to evoke atmosphere, given that performances took place in broad daylight. As indicated, props would have been kept to a minimum although the tapers would have provided part of the necessary visual shorthand to establish the nocturnal setting.

Don Pedro and Claudio are being made to play a part, but have the opportunity to write their own dialogue. Claudio, who probably penned his denunciation of Hero, has now penned an epitaph for her. He reads it out, before hanging it on the tomb:

> *Done to death by slanderous tongues*
> *Was the Hero that here lies:*
> *Death, in guerdon of her wrongs,*
> *Gives her fame which never dies.*
> *So the life that died with shame*
> *Lives in death with glorious fame.*
>
> (V. iii. 3–8)

The epitaph is depersonalized in the sense that 'slanderous tongues', rather than those who possess them, become the active agents responsible for Hero's death. It is Balthasar's song, rather than Claudio's own poem, which draws attention to the guilt of the participants themselves. Once again, Claudio appears to be in danger of tying himself up in paradoxes, in this case 'living in death' ones. *Love's Labour's Lost* opens with a speech by Navarre in which he vainly asserts that fame can live in death:

> *Let fame, that all hunt after in their lives,*
> *Live registered upon our brazen tombs,*
> *And then grace us in the disgrace of death;*
> *When, spite of cormorant devouring Time,*
> *Th'endeavour of this present breath may buy*
> *That honour which shall bate his scythe's keen edge,*
> *And make us heirs of all eternity.*
>
> (I. i. 1–7)

Navarre's belief that words, particularly written ones, can offer a permanent record or register of events is challenged throughout the play. Similarly, the dramatic context of the tomb scene in *Much Ado*, together with the paradoxical implications of this epitaph, undercut Claudio's attempts to grace the disgraced Hero. Hero lives, not because Claudio's epitaph gives her life in death, but because she has not died. The dark, sombre atmosphere of this scene symbolizes the continuation of Claudio's own inner darkness or lack of true perception about what has happened.

The scene is usually played solemnly and it is probably right to do so. Balthasar is revealed earlier on to be an appalling punster and, according to Benedick, a second-rate musician, but perhaps he is able to rise to the occasion with his hymn to Diana. This indicates that the mourners ought to circle round Hero's tomb: 'Round about her tomb they go' (V. iii. 15). Such a patterning of movement needs to be related to the staging of ceremony within the play as a whole. The opening of both the masked ball and the wedding should probably be staged in terms of circular arrangement, suggesting harmony and festivity. In both cases the real and symbolic circle is broken, most dramatically when Don Pedro and Claudio storm out of the church. Benedick's comment, before this exit, that 'This looks not like a nuptial' (IV. i. 66) can be taken quite literally. The participants have already broken the circle and rearranged themselves in such a way as to illustrate, in the visual shorthand of stage patterns, that the ceremony is broken. The formation of a new circle around Hero's tomb provides a clearer indication of repentance than do the words of the epitaph or the hymn to Diana. This circle is a reminder of the broken nuptials, but it also looks forward to the harmonious one at the end of the play.

7 Beatrice and Benedick

Introduction

Beatrice and Benedick are usually regarded as the leading roles in *Much Ado*. The poet Leonard Digges noted, by way of introduction to the 1640 edition of Shakespeare's *Poems*, how the 'cockpit, galleries, boxes, all are full' when they were on stage. Such popularity meant that the play itself often became known after its favourite parts. The financial accounts for the wedding celebrations at Whitehall in 1613 contain a reference to a play called *Benedicte and Betteris*. It has been assumed that this must be an alternative title for *Much Ado About Nothing*, which is also listed in these accounts. Charles I, who may even have attended this performance at his sister's wedding, wrote 'Benedik and Betrice' against the entry for *Much Ado About Nothing* in his Second Folio edition of the plays. This tendency to see Beatrice and Benedick as being the play itself, rather than as parts in it and of it, is taken to extremes in Hector Berlioz's comic opera *Beatrice and Benedick*, which was first performed in its completed form in 1862. Berlioz dispensed altogether with the services of Don John and Dogberry and relegated Hero and Claudio to minor roles. He filled the gap by building up the part of Balthasar into Somarone, a comic court musician. Modern theatrical interpretations of *Much Ado* never go as far as this, although the fact that Beatrice and Benedick are invariably played by the leading members of the company suggests a broadly similar approach. Beatrice and Benedick are placed at the end of this interpretation of *Much Ado* for two related reasons. First, to emphasize the point that it is dangerous to write off, or out, Don John, Don Pedro, Dogberry, Hero and Claudio as minor characters. *Much Ado* is an ensemble piece rather than just a two-hander. Secondly, to suggest that Beatrice's and Benedick's theatrical achievements can best be appreciated when they are related to the play's dramatic and thematic structure. They need to be saved from becoming just saving graces.

Pre-play relationships

Messina is a tightly-knit, claustrophobic society. Everybody either knows, or wants to know, everybody else's business. Gossip, hearsay and false report have reached epidemic proportions. The 1968 Royal Shakespeare Company production captured this enclosed, hothouse atmosphere by setting the play in a conservatory. Other modern productions have tried to convey this artificial mood through naturalistic reproductions of covered alleys, overgrown arbours and thick-pleached fruit trees. Everybody in the conservatory or walled garden appears to have world enough and time to admire cultivation, be it of fruit trees or the equally carefully nurtured wit. This society is thus also enclosed in the sense that, with the exceptions of Dogberry, Verges and the Watch, it consists of a small, leisured group and their attendants. It is, in the play's own terms, a society inhabited by people of 'sort' (I. i. 7).

The text itself provides evidence of the kind of pre-play relationships that seem inevitable in such an enclosed world. The most obvious one is perhaps between Don Pedro and Don John, whose quarrel is settled on the battlefield. Claudio and Hero have at least sighted each other. Claudio confesses to looking on her 'with a soldier's eye' (I. i. 277) before the battle. The plot to dishonour and discredit the young lovers depends upon Borachio's long-standing relationship with Margaret. Some critics accuse Shakespeare of bad craftsmanship for not developing this further. Beatrice and Benedick are obviously old sparring partners. They have their own nicknames for each other and their 'merry war' (I. i. 57) is very much a party piece. It has been suggested that a romantic pre-play relationship can be inferred from one of Beatrice's exchanges with Don Pedro:

DON PEDRO *Come, lady, come; you have lost the heart of Signor Benedick.*
BEATRICE *Indeed, my lord, he lent it me awhile, and I gave him use for it, a double heart for his single one. Marry, once before he won it of me with false dice, therefore your grace may well say I have lost it.*
DON PEDRO *You have put him down, lady, you have put him down.*
BEATRICE *So I would not he should do me, my lord, lest I should prove the mother of fools.*

(II. i. 253–62)

Such an interpretation could be supported by Don Pedro's later remark that Benedick 'hath twice or thrice cut Cupid's bow-string' (III. ii. 10), suggesting disentanglements from romantic attachments and obligations. Beatrice implies that Benedick has played her false, so these two references might be connected. It is dangerous, however, to take Beatrice's verbal sallies quite so literally. She is more interested in scoring points in these stand-up comedy routines than in offering an historically accurate survey.

Despite her own disclaimers, there is 'matter' in her 'mirth' but it is not always matter of fact. The claim that Benedick has been a lover, and a poor one at that, undercuts his cultivation of the role of confirmed bachelor and thus makes him appear ridiculous. This is Beatrice's primary purpose. She herself sounds a muffled warning against literal interpretations at the end of this exchange. Leaving aside the fairly obvious sexual meaning, one way of reading these lines is that she is putting Benedick down rhetorically before he has the chance to put her down. It is thus a fear that Benedick *will* play her false which leads to defensively aggressive jokes about how he *has* actually played her false. Benedick himself has similar anxieties about Beatrice, referring to her as 'the infernal Ate in good apparel' (II. i. 234). Ate was the Greek Goddess of Discord, so Benedick is suggesting that, although Beatrice might dress and behave like a well-brought-up lady, such outward appearances disguise her dangerous qualities. Claudio forms a similar opinion of Hero with much more disastrous consequences.

Beatrice and Benedick are certainly old campaigners, but it is unlikely that their relationship has ever taken an explicitly romantic form. Fear and anxiety mediate their statements more than a concern for truth. Also, speaking the truth is just another part to be played in this enclosed world, rather than an ultimate goal. It could be argued, at a more general level, that their relationship, like many others in the play, displays such a heightened theatricality precisely because it is of long standing. Role-play and rhetorical disguise are ways of preventing familiarity from breeding either real contempt or contented complacency. Changes of clothes and roles allow the inhabitants of this enclosed world to appear fresh and sparkling rather than contaminated and stale.

Mock ceremonial

The quarrel between Don Pedro and Don John is a petty, domestic one. Leonato and the Messenger nevertheless manage to fashion it into a chivalric contest. The sixteenth century had its own versions of the holy or just war, but these would not have included such a squabble. The opening dialogue thus deflates itself and Beatrice is on hand to complete the process. Her first question – 'I pray you, is Signor Mountanto returned from the wars, or no?' (I. i. 28–9) – immediately punctures all the hyperbole by claiming that war is a theatre for braggarts. Mountanto is probably best rendered as a swaggering swordsman. She has no patience for evasive, euphemistic celebrations of war. Leonato may ask 'how many gentlemen' have been 'lost in this action' (I. i. 5–6), but she is more direct:

I pray you, how many hath he killed and eaten in these wars? But how many hath he killed? For indeed, I promised to eat all of his killing.

(I. i. 39–41)

As far as she is concerned, the 'gentlemen' are fools and braggarts, who get 'killed' rather than merely 'lost'. She goes on to represent Benedick, whom the Messenger regards as a 'good soldier' (I. i. 49), as being no more than a self-indulgent epicure, a vain follower of fashion and an untrustworthy friend. The wider implication might be that war itself, perhaps like other supposedly courtly pursuits, produces selfishness and vanity rather than virtue and heroism.

Beatrice's disruption of this celebration of war is followed by an equally cynical approach to the welcoming ceremony. Benedick the soldier now has a real fight on his hands:

BEATRICE *I wonder that you will still be talking, Signor Benedick; nobody marks you.*
BENEDICK *What, my dear Lady Disdain! Are you yet living?*
BEATRICE *Is it possible disdain should die while she hath such meet food to feed it as Signor Benedick? Courtesy itself must convert to disdain, if you come in her presence.*
BENEDICK *Then is courtesy a turncoat. But it is certain I am loved of all ladies, only you excepted; and I would I could find in my heart that I had not a hard heart, for, truly, I love none.*

(I. i. 108–19)

The irony is, of course, that Beatrice herself 'marks' Benedick's every word and gesture. Even on the evidence of just this opening scene, it can be argued that in performance Beatrice ought to lay a heavy and unflattering stress on 'courtesy'. She is certainly not extending the most courtly of welcomes to this particular conquering hero.

Benedick's own brand of mock-ceremonial humour initially takes a different form from Beatrice's detached cynicism. He mocks courtly ceremonies by affecting to play them for real. For instance, he sets up the possibilities for a burlesque of the concept of allegiance when Don Pedro intrudes upon Claudio's confession of love:

DON PEDRO *What secret hath held you here, that you followed not to Leonato's?*
BENEDICK *I would your grace would constrain me to tell.*
DON PEDRO *I charge thee on thy allegiance.*
BENEDICK *You hear, Count Claudio; I can be secret as a dumb man, I*

> *would have you think so; but, on my allegiance, mark you*
> *this, on my allegiance – he is in love.*
>
> (I. i. 190–96)

Allegiance was a crucial aspect of the Renaissance debate on sovereignty. Subjects pledged their allegiance to the crown and, where appropriate, to the state church. The prince in turn undertook an oath of allegiance to both subjects and realm, guaranteeing protection through the rule of law. The important question, which Shakespeare dealt with extensively in his English and Roman History plays, was whether a prince could forfeit this allegiance through his own tyranny. Such weighty debates about justified resistance are alien to the 'comic climate' of *Much Ado*. Benedick, gleefully aided and abetted by the sportive Don Pedro, burlesques the issue by making it a part of a 'love-comedy game'. He also sends up notions of courtly 'service' after the masked ball. He is still feeling the effects of the rough side of Beatrice's tongue so, when he sees her approaching for the next round, begs Don Pedro to send him on a chivalric quest:

Will your grace command me any service to the world's end? I will go on the slightest errand now to the Antipodes that you can devise to send me on. I will fetch you a tooth-picker now from the furthest inch of Asia; bring you the length of Prester John's foot; fetch you a hair off the great Cham's beard; do you any embassage to the Pigmies, rather than hold three words' conference with this harpy.

(II. i. 241–8)

Benedick's string of examples, particularly the 'embassage to the Pigmies', obviously belittles the quest as a way of demonstrating allegiance. The point could be given visual weight in performance through a contrast between these comic examples and the solemnity of Benedick's accompanying gestures. It is probable that on the Elizabethan stage these would have included a 'cap and knee' routine, removing his hat and going down on one knee as a mark of homage to Prince Don Pedro.

Beatrice and Benedick both mock the ceremonies of the court in their different ways but, ultimately, neither of them represents a disruptive threat. Beatrice wounds Benedick during the masked ball by describing him as the 'Prince's jester' (II. i. 123). It may be significant that, when he first ponders her meaning, he takes this as a compliment. There is a sense in which both Beatrice and Benedick play the part of the jester or licensed fool. The jester held a permanent position in great households and was given leave, or licence, to flout social distinction and etiquette. Although some of his antics might appear to favour misrule, they were always pulled back from the brink because they carried this official sanction. Beatrice refers to the presence of such a fool in Leonato's household, but none appears. This may be another of the play's loose ends, although it is probably just an example of the way in which Beatrice sacrifices the truth to get a laugh at Benedick's expense:

He set up his bills here in Messina, and challenged Cupid at the flight; and my uncle's fool, reading the challenge, subscribed for Cupid, and challenged him at the bird-bolt.

(I. i. 36-9)

Benedick's credentials as a bachelor are, once again, called into question by claiming that he has a track record, albeit a hopeless one, as a lover. Leonato does not need to keep a resident fool because Beatrice, the disdainful lady, and Benedick, the confirmed bachelor, play the part for him and his guests. They may mock the great courtly pursuit of love, and Beatrice adds war for good measure, but are actively encouraged to do so.

The garden scenes

Beatrice and Benedick are great improvisers. The overall theme of disdain versus cynicism is neither new nor even new to *them*, so they are concerned with the quick variations that can be played upon it. They are both fast talkers who think and respond quickly on their feet in a desperate bid to have the last breathless word. Thus much of the comedy that surrounds their respective deceptions comes from the fact that these brilliant, virtuoso performers are fooled by more ordinary ones. The comedy is strengthened by the way in which both of them have made so much ado about their abilities to discern reality from illusion. Beatrice sees herself not so much as the disdainful lady as one, and the only one at that, whose perceptions are always accurate:

LEONATO   *Cousin, you apprehend passing shrewdly.*
BEATRICE   *I have a good eye, uncle; I can see a church by daylight.*

(II. i. 72–3)

Here 'shrewdly' should be taken to mean shrewishly. Such pride obviously sets up comic possibilities for a fall. Similarly, Benedick prides himself on his vision:

CLAUDIO   *In mine eye she is the sweetest lady that ever I looked on.*
BENEDICK   *I can see yet without spectacles, and I see no such matter ...*

(I. i. 175–8)

Don John and Dogberry are not alone in their obsession with self. Indeed,

Benedick's soliloquy immediately before his deception is the pinnacle of smug self-centredness from which he can only fall:

> May I be so converted and see with these eyes? I cannot tell; I think not. I will not be sworn but love may transform me to an oyster; but I'll take my oath on it, till he have made an oyster of me, he shall never make me such a fool. One woman is fair, yet I am well; another is wise, yet I am well; another virtuous, yet I am well; but till all graces be in one woman, one woman shall not come in my grace.
>
> (II. iii. 21–8)

At a more general level, both Beatrice and Benedick demonstrate their self-importance by the way in which nobody is allowed to discuss the details of the betrothal until they have had their say and then gone away.

As a few critics are puzzled by the speed with which both Beatrice and Benedick fall for the plays that are acted out for their benefit, it is worth re-emphasizing the point that *Much Ado* is concerned with 'parts' rather than with 'characters'. Beatrice and Benedick have up to this point been very self-consciously playing, and as just indicated overplaying, parts. Benedick is capable of standing outside his performance as cynical bachelor and seeing it as performance. He acknowledges to Claudio that it is his 'custom' to speak as 'a professed tyrant to their sex' (I. i. 158–9). Perhaps the clearest illustration that it is performance comes during the earlier part of his 'I am well' soliloquy when he accuses Claudio of all people of cultivating a highly rhetorical romantic pose:

> He was wont to speak plain and to the purpose, like an honest man and a soldier, and now is he turned orthography; his words are a very fantastical banquet, just so many strange dishes.
>
> (II. iii. 18–21)

The sense of 'now is he turned orthography' is that, according to Benedick, Claudio has taken to using, and perhaps even coining, an elaborate and fanciful language of love. Nothing could be further from the truth, but a performance in the role of cynic demands that young lovers have to be criticized for their ridiculous language. The fact that Claudio does not oblige does not alter Benedick's performance.

Beatrice and Benedick hear their pride and prejudices condemned whilst they are concealed in the orchard. Benedick escapes relatively lightly, although both his wit and his valour are called into question. The criticisms represent a milder version of the ones with which Beatrice launched her attack at the beginning of the play. Beatrice herself is given a much harder time of it by Hero and Ursula. All her faults have been conned by rote and are now set against her: pride, scorn and disdain. It can be argued that the speed of both Beatrice's and Benedick's conversions to love comes about through these home truths. They change because, in an unblinding flash, they acquire self-knowledge. A more widely canvassed interpretation suggests that, despite deceptive appearances, they have been in love for some time. They may appear to be obsessed by themselves, but they need each other to rail against just as lovers need each other's company. The knowledge that their love will be returned rather than scorned allays the fears and anxieties and allows them to drop the protective shell or mask. Such an interpretation has much to recommend it. Beatrice and Benedick may decide to change, however, simply because their parts have become stale and typecast. Don Pedro and Hero criticize them for the predictability of their performances. Benedick at least implies that he has been playing the part of the cynical bachelor for too long:

I may chance have some odd quirks and remnants of wit broken on me, because I have railed so long against marriage; but doth not the appetite alter? A man loves the meat in his youth that he cannot endure in his age.

(II. iii. 228–32)

The epicure may need to alter his appetite, but the actor also needs a new part after playing a familiar one for 'so long'. More tenuously, Beatrice appears to acknowledge that her performance is indeed dangerously close to over-performance: 'Stand I condemned for pride and scorn so much?' (III. i. 108). Characteristics which are meant to be part of *a* performance have been exaggerated into *the* performance.

Benedick's flouting jests at the absurdity of the lover's behaviour come home to roost with a comic vengeance as a result of his conversion. He does indeed become 'the argument of his own scorn' (II. iii. 11). He claims that he will never let love make him look pale yet, according to Don Pedro anyway, ends up exhibiting this tell-tale sign of the Elizabethan lover. The fast talker becomes tongue-tied. Benedick remains relatively silent whilst Don Pedro and Claudio, now seemingly playing the part of Benedick, mock his quick costume change. The words do not tumble out as they were wont to do. He even has to study 'eight or nine wise words' (III. ii. 65–6) to speak to Leonato. Similarly, Beatrice loses her rhetorical sharpness and is in danger of being upstaged by Margaret, who now plays the part of Beatrice the disdainful lady:

BEATRICE   *I am stuffed, cousin, I cannot smell.*
MARGARET   *A maid, and stuffed! There's goodly catching of cold.*
BEATRICE   *O, God help me! God help me! How long have you professed apprehension?*
MARGARET   *Ever since you left it. Doth not my wit become me rarely?*

BEATRICE   *It is not seen enough; you should wear it in your cap.*

(III. iv. 57–65)

Beatrice makes the punchline, but only just. She even complains at the end of this exchange about the speed or 'pace' of Margaret's tongue.

Killing Claudio

It is generally agreed that the dialogue between Beatrice and Benedick immediately after the denunciation represents one of the hardest parts of *Much Ado* to interpret both critically and theatrically. Much has been written about the correct way of delivering Beatrice's famous command 'Kill Claudio'. The problem is a genuine one, although it can be exaggerated by readings which seek to privilege one interpretation at the expense of all others. This implies that there is a single text which has a single meaning. It makes more critical sense, however, to approach *Much Ado*, on page as well as stage, as a variety of texts which therefore have a multiplicity of meanings.

Beatrice and Benedick are alone together for the first time since becoming convinced of each other's love. This suggests that the opening part of the dialogue probably needs to be played in a tentative, reticent way. This is in keeping with Beatrice's and Benedick's awkwardness in their new parts, as well as providing a marked contrast to the highly theatrical storms and furies of the denunciation itself. Benedick, like Claudio at the beginning of the play, frames his responses as questions to avoid over-committing himself:

BEATRICE   *Ah, how much might the man deserve of me that would right her!*
BENEDICK   *Is there any way to show such friendship?*
BEATRICE   *A very even way, but no such friend.*
BENEDICK   *May a man do it?*
BEATRICE   *It is a man's office, but not yours.*
BENEDICK   *I do love nothing in the world so well as you; is not that strange?*

(IV. i. 258–65)

Beatrice is hinting that Benedick ought to make a declaration of revenge, whereas he is testing out the possibilities for a declaration of love. According to purist interpretations of the revenge ethic, such retribution had to be kept within the family. Beatrice is, however, making the more general point that the ineffectual Benedick is not suitable for the 'office'. Benedick himself is in no-man's-land at this point in the play, which was a dangerous place for any courtier. He has had the courage to reject his patron, Don Pedro, by not following him out of the church. He may even have literally crossed the floor to take up a position with Beatrice and her family. Yet he still has not replaced his former allegiance with an official alliance with Beatrice. The tempo of the dialogue quickens because the participants are at cross purposes: Beatrice wants revenge, whereas Benedick will settle for a declaration of love. The tentative beginnings lead to a more familiar confrontation with each of them trying to seize and exploit the initiative. Benedick secures a declaration of love from Beatrice and appears to be in control:

BENEDICK *I protest I love thee.*
BEATRICE *Why, then, God forgive me!*
BENEDICK *What offence, sweet Beatrice?*
BEATRICE *You have stayed me in a happy hour; I was about to protest I*
          loved you.
BENEDICK *And do it with all thy heart.*
BEATRICE *I love you with so much of my heart that none is left to protest.*
                                                        (IV. i. 275–83)

Benedick holds the initiative, and in some productions Beatrice herself, at this point. His old habit of mocking courtly performances through exaggeration dies hard. His 'Come, bid me do anything for thee' (IV. i. 284) is both a throw-away and a give-away line, echoing his earlier overstated request to Don Pedro to command him 'any service'. He throws away the initiative to Beatrice who immediately calls his bluff:

BEATRICE *Kill Claudio.*
BENEDICK *Ha! Not for the wide world.*
BEATRICE *You kill me to deny it. Farewell.*
BENEDICK *Tarry, sweet Beatrice.*
BEATRICE *I am gone though I am here; there is no love in you. Nay, I pray*
          you, let me go.
BENEDICK *Beatrice –*
BEATRICE *In faith, I will go.*
                                                        (IV. i. 285–92)

Beatrice's physical rejection of Benedick – 'I pray you, let me go' – provides an inversion of the action and gestures associated with the denunciation. Claudio hands Hero back to her father, whereas Beatrice tells Benedick to keep his hands off her. This shows Beatrice's dominance and also suggests, at a more general level, that they will be unable to hold each other until Claudio has reversed his damaging gesture. This declaration of love has to be broken because the wedding has been disrupted. Beatrice's command to kill Claudio has been delivered in very strident tones, although such a theatrical interpretation stores up problems for the later speeches. The outbursts against manhood and courtliness are in danger of becoming distinctly anti-climactic, if this command is delivered near the top of the voice range. Also, it is possible to establish an effective contrast between a matter-of-fact delivery and the potentially serious nature of the command. The crescendo pitch should probably be reserved for Beatrice's virtual monologue against effeminate courtiers:

O that I were a man for his sake, or that I had any friend would be a man for my sake! But manhood is melted into curtsies, valour into compliment, and men are only turned into tongue, and trim ones too. He is now as valiant as Hercules that only tells a lie and swears it. I cannot be a man with wishing, therefore I will die a woman with grieving.

(IV. i. 312–18)

It is this onslaught, rather than the command itself, which persuades Benedick to add the part of revenger to his repertoire. He undertakes to kill more than Claudio when he picks up Beatrice's rhetorical gauntlet. He will be killing courtliness in general and thus, more particularly, the courtier in himself. He will also be striking a blow for marriage against the essentially narcissistic cult of male friendship. Claudio has to undergo a rite of passage before he is fit to enter into marriage. His critics claim that he never accomplishes this. There is obviously a discrepancy between theory and theatrical practice on this point. Claudio's trust, almost blind faith, in an unseen bride is very different from his blind rage at one whom he claims to have seen through. The problem is that, despite some of the ways in which the patterns and gestures of the finale self-consciously recall those of the denunciation scene, it is often difficult to convey this in effective theatrical terms. Claudio may come of age during the play. Benedick certainly comes to terms with his age, which means dropping the part of the self-regarding courtier.

Towards marriage

Don Pedro and Claudio still expect Benedick to continue to play the part of court jester. They make no reference to his failure to join them in their dramatic exit from the church. Perhaps they were so wrapped up in their own performances that they did not even notice his absence. They are now 'high-proof melancholy' (V. i. 122), not as a result of Hero's supposed death but because of their quarrel with Leonato and Antonio, and want to be amused. Ironically, Benedick comes to challenge Claudio to a duel but is himself challenged to a verbal duel. Don Pedro and Claudio unsuccessfully improvise witty remarks around his far from witty responses. Claudio even regards the challenge as a bit of a laugh, presumably thinking that Benedick is trying to fetch him in by adopting a mock-serious tone. Incidentally, Don Pedro is left as the on-stage audience when Benedick draws Claudio aside to issue this challenge and should be played as a particularly inquisitive one. He does not overhear it, but probably not through want of trying. Benedick, the man who would now be married, dislikes the way in which Claudio has the nerve to borrow some of his own lines to play his old part of cynical bachelor:

Fare you well, boy; you know my mind. I will leave you now to your gossip-like humour. You break jests as braggarts do their blades, which, God be thanked, hurt not. (To Don Pedro) My lord, for your many courtesies I thank you; I must discontinue your company.

(V. i. 178–83)

Besides criticizing Claudio, Benedick is offering a comment on his own performances in this part. It finally dawns on Don Pedro and Claudio that the challenger is 'in most profound earnest' (V. i. 187). The scene itself does not have to be earnest or humourless. The comedy comes largely through role reversal. Benedick, accused by Beatrice and more playfully by Don Pedro himself, of being a braggart now accuses Claudio of being one. The irony may be that Benedick, despite the attempt to play a new part, still retains some traces of the braggart. The text in general indicates that his facial gestures are very expressive. Perhaps he issues his challenge with a look which suggests what Don Pedro referred to in the garden scene as a 'most Christian-like fear' (II. iii. 190).

Benedick is ill at ease in the part of revenger and decidedly awkward as a lover. Once again, he stands outside his own performance and comments on it as performance:

Marry, I cannot show it in rhyme, I have tried; I can find out no rhyme to 'lady' but 'baby' – an innocent rhyme; for 'scorn', 'horn' – a hard rhyme; for 'school', 'fool' – a babbling rhyme; very ominous endings. No, I was not born under a rhyming planet, nor I cannot woo in festival terms.

(V. ii. 35–40)

The confession at the end of this soliloquy does not tell the theatre audience anything it does not already know. Benedick's attempts to achieve romantic sublimity are doomed to appear ridiculous. His own realization of this prompts him to tell Beatrice 'plainly' (V. ii. 52) that he has challenged Claudio. Beatrice receives the news, but seems quite happy to let Benedick initiate a playful discussion of their relationship. Perhaps this suggests that she believes that her command has been fulfilled. Benedick has, albeit in a way appropriate to the play's 'comic climate', proved his manhood and commitment. The duel itself is unimportant because he has already killed his own Claudio. Beatrice has also killed Lady Disdain. The point is made very effectively by the contrast between Benedick's dialogue with Margaret, whom he asks to send for Beatrice, and his subsequent dialogue with her. Margaret plays the part of the old Beatrice, the fast-talking, disdainful lady with a strong line in sexual innuendo:

BENEDICK *Thy wit is as quick as the greyhound's mouth; it catches.*

MARGARET *And yours as blunt as the fencer's foils, which hit, but hurt not.*

BENEDICK *A most manly wit, Margaret; it will not hurt a woman. And so, I pray thee, call Beatrice; I give thee the bucklers.*

MARGARET *Give us the swords; we have bucklers of our own.*

BENEDICK *If you use them, Margaret, you must put in the pikes with a vice; and they are dangerous weapons for maids.*

(V. ii. 11–22)

This crude variation on the theme of sexual warfare, once Beatrice's party piece, is in marked contrast to the more playfully assured tone now adopted by Beatrice and Benedick:

BENEDICK *And I pray thee now, tell me for which of my bad parts didst thou first fall in love with me?*

BEATRICE *For them all together; which maintained so politic a state of evil that they will not admit any good part to intermingle with them. But for which of my good parts did you first suffer love for me?*

BENEDICK *Suffer love! A good epithet, I do suffer love indeed, for I love thee against my will.*

BEATRICE *In spite of your heart, I think; alas, poor heart! If you spite it for my sake, I will spite it for yours; for I will never love that which my friend hates.*

BENEDICK *Thou and I are too wise to woo peaceably.*

(V. ii. 55 66)

The dialogue between Benedick and Margaret should probably be played at the frenetic, galloping pace, so characteristic of some of the earlier skirmishes of wit. Beatrice and Benedick are certainly skirmishing, but the pace of the dialogue ought to be more measured to suggest a coming to terms both with age and each other. Following on from this, it is possible to interpret the dialogue in terms of self-parody. Beatrice and Benedick act out this skirmish with a certain wry, detached amusement at their own performances. The confrontational edge, so apparent in Margaret's performance, has been replaced by mutual enjoyment. The 'I am well' or 'I am right' outlooks which they shared at the beginning of the play have changed sufficiently to allow them to mock themselves as well as each other.

It is also possible to play their betrothal in terms of assured self-parody. Thus their private dialogue can be seen as a rehearsal for this public event. Benedick appears not to have tumbled to the fact that his new relationship with Beatrice is based on honest deception or slander. Leonato drops a very heavy hint about the garden scenes, but he finds this 'enigmatical' (V. iv. 27). It is therefore doubtful, although not impossible given the deceptive nature of appearances in the play, that Benedick is deliberately trying to make his deceivers feel uncomfortable when he mentions how he became convinced of Beatrice's love. He probably introduces the ironic notion of the deceivers themselves being deceived as part of a more general ploy whereby he and Beatrice will continue to parody themselves to the very end. He has rejected 'festival terms' and returned, tongue very firmly in cheek, to the part of reluctant bachelor. Beatrice follows suit by being playfully offhand about his suit. Claudio and Hero call their theatrical bluff by producing the sonnets that they have written to each other. They nevertheless insist on playing out their self-parody to the end:

BENEDICK *A miracle! Here's our own hands against our hearts. Come, I will have thee; but, by this light, I take thee for pity.*

BEATRICE *I would not deny you; but, by this good day, I yield upon great persuasion; and partly to save your life, for I was told you were in a consumption.*

BENEDICK (kissing her) *Peace! I will stop your mouth.*

(V. iv. 91–7)

According to neo-platonic theory the kiss represented a perfect union of body and soul as the mouth was a part of the body as well as being 'a channel for words, which are the interpreters of the soul, and for human breath or spirit', as Pietro Bembo puts it towards the end of *The Courtier*. This kiss, which Benedick had been unable to take until the discord caused by Claudio was resolved, symbolizes a wider harmony. Similarly, the dance with which the play ends signals the triumph of harmonious order over comic chaos.

The kiss is, however, open to a more prosaic and potentially more disturbing interpretation: the voluble lady finally has her mouth stopped. Whereas Benedick becomes a noisy and rather domineering master of ceremonies during the closing moments of the play, Beatrice is not given another word to speak. This is how it appears on the page, although on the stage she can play a full part in these final festivities. It has to be said, nevertheless, that such a part is a subordinate or supporting one. Although the taming of the disdainful lady would have been seen by Elizabethan audiences as a crucial aspect of this final harmony, it can strike a more discordant note with present-day ones. Beatrice was potentially more subversive than Benedick in the role of court jester. Her terms of reference were wider, including war as well as love, and her detachment from some of the courtly ceremonies and rituals more threatening than Benedick's over-playing of them. She was, in short, more of a danger because she was a woman who criticized masculine values. Her outburst to Benedick against ineffective, narcissistic courtiers after the denunciation is a particularly damning one. Its dramatic context, however, suggests that she needs to be seen as a tamer as well as somebody who is tamed. She forces an initially reluctant Benedick to abandon some of the more self-regarding aspects of courtiership. In a play in which the men make much ado about loyalty, it is her unswerving loyalty to Hero which makes the deepest impression, as well as providing the most lasting criticism of courtliness. The 'comic climate' of *Much Ado*, and the social and cultural climate of Elizabethan England to which it is linked, demand that the disdainful lady should be tamed. It could be argued that *Much Ado*, like many of Shakespeare's other comedies, seems unable or even unwilling to incorporate potentially radical possibilities and opportunities within a conservative resolution, which thus becomes at best fragile and at worst deeply ambivalent. This makes some sense as a general proposition. It needs to be qualified, however, by an awareness of the fact that for Elizabethan audiences the institution of marriage, and the cult of 'chaste constancy' upon which it was based, were not necessarily equated with conservative resolutions. Indeed, the reverse may well have been true. Marriage could be modern and progressive, if not fundamentally radical, because it represented a challenge to the established institution of courtiership. In other words, Elizabethan audiences would probably not have noticed such a discrepancy between Beatrice's critique of courtiers and her eventual marriage to a reformed one.

Selected bibliography

R. A. Foakes's New Penguin Shakespeare edition contains a very useful descriptive reading list. The best detailed account of the play is J. R. Mulryne's *Shakespeare: Much Ado About Nothing* (Edward Arnold, 1965). Anthologies of criticism include:

John Russell Brown (ed.): *Shakespeare: Much Ado About Nothing and As You Like It* (Macmillan, 1979).
W. R. Davis (ed.): *Twentieth Century Interpretations of Much Ado About Nothing* (Prentice Hall Inc., 1969).

1) Shakespearean comedy

C. L. Barber: *Shakespeare's Festive Comedy: A Study of Dramatic Form in Relation to Social Custom* (Princeton University Press, 1972).
Muriel Bradbrook: *The Growth and Structure of Elizabethan Comedy* (Chatto, 1961).
Malcolm Bradbury and David Palmer (eds): *Shakespearian Comedy* (Edward Arnold, 1972).
Northrop Frye: *A Natural Perspective: The Development of Shakespearean Comedy and Romance* (Harcourt, Brace & World Inc., 1965).

2) Stage and staging

David Bevington: *Action is Eloquence: Shakespeare's Language of Gesture* (Harvard University Press, 1984).
Andrew Gurr: *The Shakespearean Stage 1574–1642* (Cambridge University Press, 1980).
Michael Hattaway: *Elizabethan Popular Theatre: Plays in Performance* (Routledge and Kegan Paul, 1982).
Ann Pasternak Slater: *Shakespeare the Director* (Harvester Press, 1982).

3) Contexts

Geoffrey Bullough (ed.): *Narrative and Dramatic Sources of Shakespeare: Volume Two, The Comedies 1597–1603* (Routledge and Kegan Paul, 1968).

Rosalie Colie: *Paradoxica Epidemica: The Renaissance Tradition of Paradox* (Archon, 1976).

Juliet Dusinberre: *Shakespeare and the Nature of Women* (Macmillan, 1975).

G. B. Harrison (ed.): *The Elizabethan Journals: Being a Record of Those Things Most Talked of During the Years 1591–1603* (Routledge and Kegan Paul, 1955).

Lisa Jardine: *Still Harping on Daughters: Women and Drama in the Age of Shakespeare* (Harvester Press, 1983).

H. Koenigsberger: *The Government of Sicily under Philip II of Spain* - (Staples Press Ltd, 1951).

J. L. Lievsay: *The Elizabethan Image of Italy* (Cornell University Press, 1964).

Gerald Mast: *The Comic Mind: Comedy and the Movies* (Chicago University Press, 1979).

Mario Praz: 'Shakespeare's Italy', *Shakespeare Survey*, 7, 1954.

C. T. Prouty: *The Sources of Much Ado About Nothing* (Yale University Press, 1950).

W. A. Rebhorn: *Courtly Performances: Masking and Festivity in Castiglione's Book of the Courtier* (Wayne State University Press, 1978).

Quentin Skinner: *The Foundations of Modern Political Thought*, two vols (Cambridge University Press, 1978).

4) Texts

J. F. Cox: 'The Stage Representation of the "Kill Claudio" Sequence in *Much Ado About Nothing*', *Shakespeare Survey*, 32, 1979.

Marilyn French: *Shakespeare's Division of Experience* (Sphere, 1983).

Janice Hays: '"Those Soft and Delicate Desires": *Much Ado* and the Distrust of Women', in Carolyn Lenz *et al* (eds), *The Woman's Part: Feminist Criticism of Shakespeare* (University of Illinois Press, 1980).

Richard Henze: 'Deception in Much Ado', *Studies in English Literature*, XI, 1971.

A. R. Humphreys: Introduction to the Arden Edition of *Much Ado About Nothing* (Methuen, 1981).

Arthur Kirsch: *Shakespeare and the Experience of Love* (Cambridge University Press, 1981).

Elliot Krieger: 'Social Relations and the Social Order in *Much Ado About Nothing*', *Shakespeare Survey*, 32, 1979.

Alexander Leggatt: *Shakespeare's Comedy of Love* (Methuen, 1974).

Ruth Nevo: *Comic Transformations in Shakespeare* (Methuen, 1980).

Selected bibliography

Peter G. Phiales: *Shakespeare's Romantic Comedies: The Development of Their Form and Meaning* (University of North Carolina Press, 1966).

A. P. Rossiter: *Angel with Horns: Fifteen Lectures on Shakespeare* (Longman, 1961).

David Lloyd Stevenson: *The Love-Game Comedy* (AMS Press Inc., 1966).

FOR THE BEST IN PAPERBACKS, LOOK FOR THE

In every corner of the world, on every subject under the sun, Penguin represents quality and variety – the very best in publishing today.

For complete information about books available from Penguin – including Pelicans, Puffins, Peregrines and Penguin Classics – and how to order them, write to us at the appropriate address below. Please note that for copyright reasons the selection of books varies from country to country.

In the United Kingdom: Please write to *Dept E.P., Penguin Books Ltd, Harmondsworth, Middlesex, UB7 0DA*

If you have any difficulty in obtaining a title, please send your order with the correct money, plus ten per cent for postage and packaging, to *PO Box No 11, West Drayton, Middlesex*

In the United States: Please write to *Dept BA, Penguin, 299 Murray Hill Parkway, East Rutherford, New Jersey 07073*

In Canada: Please write to *Penguin Books Canada Ltd, 2801 John Street, Markham, Ontario L3R 1B4*

In Australia: Please write to the *Marketing Department, Penguin Books Australia Ltd, P.O. Box 257, Ringwood, Victoria 3134*

In New Zealand: Please write to the *Marketing Department, Penguin Books (NZ) Ltd, Private Bag, Takapuna, Auckland 9*

In India: Please write to *Penguin Overseas Ltd, 706 Eros Apartments, 56 Nehru Place, New Delhi, 110019*

In Holland: Please write to *Penguin Books Nederland B.V., Postbus 195, NL–1380AD Weesp, Netherlands*

In Germany: Please write to *Penguin Books Ltd, Friedrichstrasse 10–12, D–6000 Frankfurt Main 1, Federal Republic of Germany*

In Spain: Please write to *Longman Penguin España, Calle San Nicolas 15, E–28013 Madrid, Spain*

In France: Please write to *Penguin Books Ltd, 39 Rue de Montmorency, F-75003, Paris, France*

In Japan: Please write to *Longman Penguin Japan Co Ltd, Yamaguchi Building, 2–12–9 Kanda Jimbocho, Chiyoda-Ku, Tokyo 101, Japan*

PENGUIN CLASSICS

Saint Anselm	**The Prayers and Meditations**
Saint Augustine	**The Confessions**
Bede	**A History of the English Church and People**
Chaucer	**The Canterbury Tales**
	Love Visions
	Troilus and Criseyde
Froissart	**The Chronicles**
Geoffrey of Monmouth	**The History of the Kings of Britain**
Gerald of Wales	**History and Topography of Ireland**
	The Journey through Wales and The Description of Wales
Gregory of Tours	**The History of the Franks**
Julian of Norwich	**Revelations of Divine Love**
William Langland	**Piers the Ploughman**
Sir John Mandeville	**The Travels of Sir John Mandeville**
Marguerite de Navarre	**The Heptameron**
Christine de Pisan	**The Treasure of the City of Ladies**
Marco Polo	**The Travels**
Richard Rolle	**The Fire of Love**
Thomas à Kempis	**The Imitation of Christ**

ANTHOLOGIES AND ANONYMOUS WORKS

The Age of Bede
Alfred the Great
Beowulf
A Celtic Miscellany
The Cloud of Unknowing and Other Works
The Death of King Arthur
The Earliest English Poems
Early Christian Writings
Early Irish Myths and Sagas
Egil's Saga
The Letters of Abelard and Heloise
Medieval English Verse
Njal's Saga
Seven Viking Romances
Sir Gawain and the Green Knight
The Song of Roland

FOR THE BEST IN PAPERBACKS, LOOK FOR THE 🐧

PENGUIN CLASSICS

Benjamin Disraeli	**Sybil**
George Eliot	**Adam Bede**
	Daniel Deronda
	Felix Holt
	Middlemarch
	The Mill on the Floss
	Romola
	Scenes of Clerical Life
	Silas Marner
Elizabeth Gaskell	**Cranford and Cousin Phillis**
	The Life of Charlotte Brontë
	Mary Barton
	North and South
	Wives and Daughters
Edward Gibbon	**The Decline and Fall of the Roman Empire**
George Gissing	**New Grub Street**
Edmund Gosse	**Father and Son**
Richard Jefferies	**Landscape with Figures**
Thomas Macaulay	**The History of England**
Henry Mayhew	**Selections from London Labour and The London Poor**
John Stuart Mill	**On Liberty**
William Morris	**News from Nowhere and Selected Writings and Designs**
Walter Pater	**Marius the Epicurean**
John Ruskin	**'Unto This Last' and Other Writings**
Sir Walter Scott	**Ivanhoe**
Robert Louis Stevenson	**Dr Jekyll and Mr Hyde**
William Makepeace Thackeray	**The History of Henry Esmond**
	Vanity Fair
Anthony Trollope	**Barchester Towers**
	Framley Parsonage
	Phineas Finn
	The Warden
Mrs Humphrey Ward	**Helbeck of Bannisdale**
Mary Wollstonecraft	**Vindication of the Rights of Woman**

FOR THE BEST IN PAPERBACKS, LOOK FOR THE 🐧

PENGUIN CLASSICS

Arnold Bennett	**The Old Wives' Tale**
Joseph Conrad	**Heart of Darkness**
	Nostromo
	The Secret Agent
	The Shadow-Line
	Under Western Eyes
E. M. Forster	**Howard's End**
	A Passage to India
	A Room With a View
	Where Angels Fear to Tread
Thomas Hardy	**The Distracted Preacher and Other Tales**
	Far From the Madding Crowd
	Jude the Obscure
	The Mayor of Casterbridge
	The Return of the Native
	Tess of the d'Urbervilles
	The Trumpet Major
	Under the Greenwood Tree
	The Woodlanders
Henry James	**The Aspern Papers** and **The Turn of the Screw**
	The Bostonians
	Daisy Miller
	The Europeans
	The Golden Bowl
	An International Episode and Other Stories
	Portrait of a Lady
	Roderick Hudson
	Washington Square
	What Maisie Knew
	The Wings of the Dove
D. H. Lawrence	**The Complete Short Novels**
	The Plumed Serpent
	The Rainbow
	Selected Short Stories
	Sons and Lovers
	The White Peacock
	Women in Love

FOR THE BEST IN PAPERBACKS, LOOK FOR THE

PENGUIN CLASSICS

Horatio Alger, Jr.	**Ragged Dick** and **Struggling Upward**
Phineas T. Barnum	**Struggles and Triumphs**
Ambrose Bierce	**The Enlarged Devil's Dictionary**
Kate Chopin	**The Awakening and Selected Stories**
Stephen Crane	**The Red Badge of Courage**
Richard Henry Dana, Jr.	**Two Years Before the Mast**
Frederick Douglass	**Narrative of the Life of Frederick Douglass, An American Slave**
Theodore Dreiser	**Sister Carrie**
Ralph Waldo Emerson	**Selected Essays**
Joel Chandler Harris	**Uncle Remus**
Nathaniel Hawthorne	**Blithedale Romance**
	The House of the Seven Gables
	The Scarlet Letter and Selected Tales
William Dean Howells	**The Rise of Silas Lapham**
Alice James	**The Diary of Alice James**
William James	**Varieties of Religious Experience**
Jack London	**The Call of the Wild and Other Stories**
	Martin Eden
Herman Melville	**Billy Budd, Sailor and Other Stories**
	Moby-Dick
	Redburn
	Typee
Thomas Paine	**Common Sense**
Edgar Allan Poe	**The Narrative of Arthur Gordon Pym of Nantucket**
	The Other Poe
	The Science Fiction of Edgar Allan Poe
	Selected Writings
Harriet Beecher Stowe	**Uncle Tom's Cabin**
Henry David Thoreau	**Walden** and **Civil Disobedience**
Mark Twain	**The Adventures of Huckleberry Finn**
	A Connecticut Yankee at King Arthur's Court
	Life on the Mississippi
	Pudd'nhead Wilson
	Roughing It